T0015373

The Populist Moment

The Jacobin series features short interrogations of politics, economics, and culture from a socialist perspective, as an avenue to radical political practice. The books offer critical analysis and engagement with the history and ideas of the Left in an accessible format.

The series is a collaboration between Verso Books and *Jacobin* magazine, which is published quarterly in print and online at jacobinmag.com.

Other titles in this series from Verso Books include:

Four Futures by Peter Frase
Class War by Megan Erickson
Building the Commune by George Ciccariello-Maher
People's Republic of Walmart by
Leigh Phillips and Michal Rozworski
Red State Revolt by Eric Blanc
Capital City by Samuel Stein
Without Apology by Jenny Brown
All-American Nativism by Daniel Denvir
A Planet to Win by Kate Aronoff, Alyssa Battistoni,
Daniel Aldana Cohen, and Thea Riofrancos
Toward Freedom by Touré F. Reed

The Populist Moment

The Left after the Great Recession

ARTHUR BORRIELLO
and ANTON JÄGER

VERSO

London • New York

First published by Verso 2023
© Arthur Borriello and Anton Jäger 2023

Sections of this book draw on these previously published coauthored articles:
"Making Sense of Populism," *Catalyst*, Winter 2020; "From Bowling Alone to Posting Alone", *Jacobin*, December 5, 2022; "Is Left Populism the Solution?," *Jacobin*, March 31, 2019; "Italy's Five Falling Stars," *Jacobin*, September 26, 2019; "We Bet the House on Left Populism—and Lost," *Jacobin*, November 25, 2019; "The *Guardian*'s Populism Panic," *Jacobin*, December 5, 2018; "On the Front Lines of the Populism Wars," *Jacobin*, June 8, 2018; and "The Myth of Populism," *Jacobin*, January 3, 2018.

All rights reserved

The moral rights of the authors have been asserted

1 3 5 7 9 10 8 6 4 2

Verso
UK: 6 Meard Street, London W1F 0EG
US: 388 Atlantic Avenue, Brooklyn, NY 11217
versobooks.com

Verso is the imprint of New Left Books

ISBN-13: 978-1-80429-248-8
ISBN-13: 978-1-80429-243-3 (UK EBK)
ISBN-13: 978-1-80429-247-1 (US EBK)

British Library Cataloguing in Publication Data
A catalogue record for this book is available from the British Library

Library of Congress Cataloging-in-Publication Data

Names: Borriello, Arthur author. | Jäger, Anton, 1994– author.
Title: The populist moment : the Left after the great recession / Arthur Borriello and Anton Jäger.
Description: First paperback edition | London ; New York : Verso, 2023. | Series: Jacobin | Includes bibliographical references.
Identifiers: LCCN 2023016777 (print) | LCCN 2023016778 (ebook) | ISBN 9781804292488 (paperback) | ISBN 9781804292471 (US ebk)
Subjects: LCSH: Populism. | Right and left (Political science)
Classification: LCC JC423 .B654 2023 (print) | LCC JC423 (ebook) | DDC 320.56/62—dc23/eng/20230511
LC record available at https://lccn.loc.gov/2023016777
LC ebook record available at https://lccn.loc.gov/2023016778

Typeset in Fournier MT by Hewer Text UK Ltd, Edinburgh
Printed and bound by CPI Group (UK) Ltd, Croydon CR0 4YY

CONTENTS

INTRODUCTION:
THE LONG 2010S

Over seven years ago, in the sweltering summer of 2015, British journalist Paul Mason found himself in a state of uncontrollable excitement. He was standing in the middle of Athens's Syntagma Square, surrounded by thousands of Greek protesters chanting songs and slogans from the country's fight against the dictatorship in the 1970s. Up on stage he could see the Syriza head and Greek president, Alexis Tsipras, leader of a six-month-old government now mired in a protracted battle with European authorities. Tsipras had been campaigning for a "no" vote in the referendum scheduled for the next day, launched as the final move in his standoff with the Eurogroup and the International Monetary Fund (IMF). Mason in turn had been chronicling Syriza's travails for the British Channel 4, informing followers on Twitter and Facebook and drafting rousing columns for the *Guardian*. On the night of Syriza's election victory on January 6, 2015, Mason inserted a short reply to a tweet by American adult actress Jessica Stoyadinovich (or "Stoya"), who had briefly mentioned the Greek drama: "Stoya," Mason exclaimed ecstatically, "come to Athens, the revolution is happening!"

Seven years later, Mason was engaged in a different set of practices. In early 2022, he had begun emailing contacts in British secret services with info on members of the UK Labour Party who had left the party after Jeremy Corbyn's defeat in the 2019 parliamentary elections. Having sided with Corbyn's successor, Keir Starmer, Mason worried that remaining Corbynites in the party would push a pro-Russian line following Putin's invasion of Ukraine. Mason's messages signaled the twilight of an entire epoch: from populist enthusiast to aspiring counter-intelligence informant, from Syntagma to Whitehall.

Mason's conversion also marks the close of an era: the period of "left populism," when left-wing parties and movements across the West—some old, some new—initiated a populist turn. The story of that era is closely tied to the twists and turns of Mason's rapturous decade. The "long 2010s," running roughly from 2008 to 2022, were as tumultuous as they were confusing. In 2015, Mason and others hoped that Syriza would "bring down the international financial system" and build a social Europe. Syriza's fall from grace was followed by listless poll numbers for Mélenchon in France, Sanders's defeat in the US, Podemos's struggles in Spain, Die Linke's crisis in Germany, and Corbyn's rout in the UK. By the close of the 2010s, practically all the populist powers were out of power. Podemos failed to negotiate a coalition with the Spanish socialists in 2019, only to end up as a junior partner in the same social democratic government a few months later. Collapsing opinion polls, uneasy anti-Macron antics, and electoral scandals in turn made La France insoumise dither, before eventually adopting a more classical left-wing identity in the 2022 election. German experiments with left-wing populism in the Aufstehen move-ment never properly got off the ground. Corbyn's Labour brutally crashed in the December 2019 election. And after a second run in 2020, Bernie Sanders once again lost to a Democratic Party insider.

All these forces took part in the political cycle spawned by the 2007–08 financial crisis, which metastasized from the United States to Europe. All hoped to rethink and revive the left by adopting a populist identity—either through the installation of new, dynamic party machines or by the capture of existing sclerotic parties. The hopes invested in this moment were considerable: by the middle of the decade, they were stirring both Mason's libido and the dreams of thousands of young activists all across the West. But as the world crept out of its COVID winter sleep in 2022, the populist left appeared as a sullen and spent force. What had happened?

This book ventures an answer to that question. Covering the period from 2008 to 2022, it investigates and assesses the left's experiments with populist politics, from Europe to the United States, offering a panoramic view of the moment's origins, strengths and weaknesses, and conjecturing where the left—and populism—might be headed from here.

The left's populist episode ran across two interlocking time-lines, punctuated by different, but related, crises. The first timeline corresponds to the 2008 crash, which disturbed and, in certain instances, demolished the established party systems across the West and its periphery. From there, an economic crisis thus morphed into a *political* crisis. The second covers the older erosion and eventual implosion of party democracy across the Atlantic since the mid-1970s, in which parties hemorrhaged members, formed cartels with other parties, or steadily forfeited their powers of state. For the left, this transition from mass to cartel parties was laden with ambiguity. On the one hand, it generated real opportunities for radicals to soak up and appeal to disaffected voters who could no longer voice their discontent within established political parties. Yet it also heavily constrained the space in which left-wing politics itself could take place. The social landscape sculpted by neoliberal reforms meant not just a disaffection from traditional parties but a retreat from the public sphere altogether, with the new medium of the internet now serving as a repository for the resulting anger and alienation. Left populists were tasked with mobilizing these now profoundly demobilized societies. More dramatically, they now were forced to build a left without a muscular labor movement.

The first sign of this populist shift was audible in the rhetoric of the parties themselves. From 2012 onwards, invocation of the "people" became a central motif for left-wing parties, both old and new. This adoption of a cross-class language of the "people" was hardly a novelty for the left, particularly in Latin America. The theorists most strongly associated with it—thinkers such as the Argentinian philosopher Ernesto Laclau and the Belgian political theorist Chantal Mouffe—had drafted their theses decades ago. In Europe, they finally found a new, real-world utility beyond academia.

Yet their "populism" also took a highly specific organizational form in the 2010s, both in Europe and the United States. Instead of the mass parties of the twentieth century, leftists were faced with a profoundly demobilized civil society which had driven citizens out of politics altogether, rendering the relations between elites and citizens highly volatile. The twin crises of the 2010s thus confronted the left with a twin set of dilemmas. The first dilemma concerned a question of substance. What was the natural base for a left-wing program, both in terms of its composition and the conditions for its mobilization? The second dilemma was one of form, and had to do with the more recent and vexing story of mass demobilization.

This first puzzle had always assumed a particular shape for twentieth-century social democrats. As the Polish American political scientist Adam Przeworski saw it, there was a clear point of departure at which left-wing parties would trade talk of the "working class" for that of the "people." In his view, the scenario ran as follows: on the one hand, early twentieth-century social democrats hoped that the expansion of industry would usher in a de facto working-class majority, which would allow them to capture office and reform their way into socialism. On the other hand, the continuing stagnation and eventual shrinkage of the class in question generated a further dilemma. Broadening the base would require concessions to middle-class constituencies, who had to remain the primary funders of the welfare state and use the same public services as the classes below them. On the other hand, the more benefits were granted to the middle classes in terms of consumer goods, the less breathing room for domestic industry, and the material bases of working-class strength and support would wither. Hence the tough choices laid out by Przeworski.[1]

Przeworski's dilemma elicited a shifting set of answers across the history of social democracy. For the German party theorist Karl Kautsky, for instance, it implied a policy of land redistribution to appease German peasants. For a reformist such as his compatriot Eduard Bernstein, it meant a tactical alliance between the new middle classes and the working classes—a bridge built from office to factory. For the Italian Marxist Antonio Gramsci, it meant reaching out to Italy's Southern peasantry, held in check by the fascist state and the industrial North. For French thinkers such as Serge Mallet and André Gorz, in turn, it meant a focus on students rather than on the industrial proletariat of yesterday. All these positions already exhibited a populist temptation, trading "the working class" for "the people."[2] A rival tradition opted for a different tactic altogether. Rather than acting in the name of the working class, American and Russian populists in the late nineteenth century consciously represented a "people" of small property owners and farmers who sought to secure political rather than economic democracy.

Whichever tradition one chose, there was no denying that populism and socialism shared a bloodline. Unlike European social democracy, populism in the United States first blossomed in neither the city nor the company town: it sprang out of the Great Plains and the rural South, in a post-plantation economy dragged into the vortex of the global cotton market. Falling prices, high railroad fees, rural debt, and corporate malfeasance fueled its rise, coupled with early suffrage extension and large networks of Protestant churches. American socialism built upon this rural heritage, although it displaced the center of gravity to more urban elements. Even the American Bolshevik journalist John Reed conceded populism's merits. In 1912, he claimed that it "had always been on the side of democracy," mainly when defending policies such as the "destruction of private monopoly and the referendum."[3]

The relative symbiosis between populism and socialism did not go unnoticed in Europe. Kautsky, Europe's "pope of Marxism," celebrated the American agrarian's rebellious attitude and looked forward to the day that "American farmers and wage workers would be welded together into one party."[4] All of this spoke in favor of a populist-socialist rapprochement. The degree of consonance was never clear, however. Attempts at populist-socialist coalitions often foundered on questions of ideology and organization, or personal politics.

These questions returned with a vengeance in the twenty-first century. In the 2010s, left parties once again had to weld together an older working class with a middle class squeezed by the credit crisis. Most started with the latter and moved toward the former, generating several dilemmas along the way. Yet in the 2010s the composition of those two groups was vastly different from the working and middle classes that socialists had sought to unite in the nineteenth and twentieth centuries, with workers now driven not only out of the factory but also out of the public sphere itself. This spawned a second and even more vexing conundrum for the populist left. In short: How was it to respond and organize against the secular impoverishment of political life since the 1970s, and what opportunities, if any, could it truly offer?

This in turn only exacerbated the dilemma that had haunted social democracy from the start. While social democrats classically had an industrial working class and middle class to work with, left populists could assume neither of these two groups. Instead, the deindustrialization and ensuing crisis of civil society of the 1980s opened a void between citizens and states, while radically decoupling Western elites from their own societies. Working-class people in particular stopped voting and abandoned political parties. These groups' respective political attitudes also shifted significantly. While an internationally oriented working class had faced a nationalist middle class throughout the twentieth century, these categories had now switched sides: the working class became tied to national welfare states, while the middle class looked for the benefits in globalization.[5] This void dislocated the parameters of left-wing politics in an even more disorientating way: in a disorganized democracy in which politics itself was in crisis, the left's organizational goals appeared tenuous at best, and unrealistic at worst.[6] Hence the resort to a populist strategy from *within* the left: to rethink mobilization for an age of demobilization; to organize for an age of disorganization. As we shall see, the populist turn was part of a crisis of social democracy itself—an attempt to *replace* social democracy rather than abolish it.

This was no easy task, and, in the end, their attempt to accomplish this transformation put leftists in a crippling double bind. They would go "full" populist, reaching the wider base of citizens driven out from politics and disaffected by social democracy. At the same time, this approach risked hollowing out the left's historic identity and commitments. Eschewing this strategy also meant a heavily digital top-down approach to coalition building. Finally, such a strategy might not grant the left enough organizational heft to face down the forces of capital on their own terrain. On the other hand, falling back on a classical left-wing identity might also scare off predominantly middle-class voters whose loyalty to the left's program was fading. Partly because of the latter's embrace of the Third Way—social democracy's conversion to a pro-market agenda in the 1990s—and the demands of the post-2008 austerity program, any return to this tradition had become a liability. Once again, the trade-off between the middle and working class that had troubled social democracy from the beginning now found a new incarnation in the trade-off between a populist and a socialist approach. The dilemma of form and the dilemma of content thus presented the populist left with two binaries. Each side of the binary came with its own disadvantages— both were, in their own way, equally undesirable. For the first dilemma, they could go for a majoritarian yet predominantly middle-class movement or a minoritarian yet purely working-class party. For the second, they could opt for an ideologically pure but politically inflexible left-wing approach or a highly versatile and hollow populist one. Reshuffling the first, the second dilemma was intimately tied to the crisis of political engagement so specific to the twenty-first century.

The long-term erosion of these center-left parties thus laid the groundwork for the "populist explosion." So when and how exactly did it finally detonate? Here, the left's populist moment possessed more recent roots. Although the 2008 crisis initially took off in the United States, its fallout quickly reached Europe, toppling private banks that had engaged in risky overseas lending and now began to appeal to governments for help. With liquidity bound up in their banking sector, several European countries opted for draconian austerity measures that decimated their public sectors. In the United States, the effects of crisis-fighting pushed a generation into debt dependency and low wages, and yet growth rates did not implode. In Southern Europe and the UK, however, a doom loop between private and public balance sheets drove the economy further downhill and discredited ruling center-left parties. Faced with a shrinking public sector and dwindling job prospects, millennials disillusioned with neoliberalism began to radicalize. Austerity continued unabated, however, as the measures in question were accepted by the political class; both die-hard conservatives and social democrats found themselves toeing the austerian line. Like the economic crises that befell the first populists in the 1880s, a second Gilded Age had now opened.[7]

As an early response, people flocked to squares in several Western cities throughout 2010 and 2011, both in Europe and the States. Known as the "Indignados" in Spain, "Occupy" in the US, "tuition protesters" in the UK, and the "Aganaktismenoi" in Greece, these leaderless movements tickled the popular imagination. Yet they offered only a hazy path forward and had no clear civil-society infrastructure behind them. The upsurge in Spain, for example, relied on spontaneous gatherings by students and workers reading out testimonies of the crisis, and refused to spell out an explicit set of demands. In Greece, protesters set fire to a Christmas tree and almost stormed parliament—powerful demonstrations of discontent, but lacking a clear road map for change. For the left, such tactics had obvious limits. Center-left parties proved incapable of camouflaging their sell-out using the PR tactics generalized in the 2000s. By 2012, it was clear that the Indignados could not sustain another march and that energy on the ground was fading. "The crisis is not enough," said one activist in 2012, disappointed by the antipolitical bent the protests had taken. Without an identifiable leadership, the movement would quickly fall prey to demagogues and cynics or get sucked into the nationalist maelstrom that was fast engulfing the West.

Academia provided an unexpected boost here. On the other side of the barricades, Ernesto Laclau became an evangelist for figures within Syriza, Podemos, and La France insoumise. Although Laclau passed away in 2014, shortly before Europe's populist moment peaked, he had impeccable credentials—he had been close to Hugo Chávez and supportive of Argentina's Kirchner government in the early 2000s. Since his so-called post-Marxist turn in the early 1980s, Laclau had urged the European left to abandon antiquated references to "class." Instead, he sent them out into the streets with a new cleavage: peoples versus elites.[8]

There were clear preconditions for Laclau's sudden relevance. Traditional European party politics was experiencing a historic crisis, exemplified by the complete inability of the Greek Social Democratic Party (Pasok) to advance any alternative to the Euro-Diktats. "Pasokification" quickly became a general metaphor for the center-left's delegitimation in the crater of 2008. In the years leading up to the crisis, European parties had steadily disengaged from their social bases, increasingly resorting to PR and marketing techniques. The fact that citizens spontaneously turned to protest marches in 2011 showed how limited the repertoire had become. Their options ranged from the referendum and the street riot to spamming pages on Facebook. In contrast to the mass party, the new left populism thus found itself uncomfortably spread across an amalgam of groups. On the one hand, the credit crisis affected older post-industrial workers, who had been hit hard by the recession in Western countries and remained generally tied to their national welfare states. Since the stripping out of communist parties, they either stopped voting or were seduced by new nationalist formations.

Figures such as Jean-Luc Mélenchon in France, Bernie Sanders in the United States, and Pablo Iglesias in Spain were always forthright about their desire to shepherd this group of voters back to the left. This was expressed in slogans such as Mélenchon's *"Fâchés mais pas fachos"* (furious but not fascists), or the goal of Iglesias's colleague Íñigo Errejón to move "beyond left and right." The chief skeptics of this strategy belonged to that other group of voters targeted by the populist left: young, networked, and educated millennials with high digital proficiency. Most of them graduated from university and were dropped into the overcrowded labor market of the 2010s. Many ended up in a stagnant service sector. Faced with a steadily digitalizing public sphere, freed from the shackles of the "old media," most of these voters were indeed ripe for radicalization. (When Tsipras was elected in 2015, he counted about 30 percent of Greek youth among his supporters.)

But their views did not always match those of the older, more traditional working-class constituencies that left-wing populists held close to their hearts. This became all too apparent in Jeremy Corbyn's Labour Party, where a shaky coalition of working-class people in the North and urban millennials in the South began to fracture over the Brexit issue. A disjunction with the remaining post-industrial working class, together with an overly fluid party structure, meant that it was almost impossible to muster a majoritarian coalition. The age-old dilemma of social democracy ("working class" versus "middle class") was now superimposed on the new organizational dilemma of the 2010s ("either too left or too populist").

Left-wing populism therefore found itself in a trap. It proved too left-wing to take full advantage of the collapse of the traditional party system; on the other hand, it was also too populist ("trapped in its hypothesis") to answer the organizational question.[9] Other forces provide an instructive contrast here. Parties such as the Italian Five Star Movement—far from conservative but hardly socialist either—were always eager to transcend the left–right divide and adopt a "catch-all" approach. Yet while Cinque Stelle tried its hand at catching everything, it now caught nothing at all. Podemos, on the other hand, was repeatedly overtaken by its far-left background, and stigmatized by opponents as "communist." The degree of this stigma varied, however, and none of the left-populist bids after 2008 ever assumed a uniform shape. Conditioned by the electoral system and the nature of post-2008 crisis management, left populists arose either inside or outside of parties, took over existing parties or started new ones, and displayed highly divergent relations to the protest movements that preceded and accompanied them.

Taking stock of today's populism as a product of the 2010s also necessitates freeing ourselves from a mindset we've inherited from an earlier age—one that insists our world is currently in the grip of a "fascist" resurgence. In the six years since Donald Trump's election, a waspish debate on whether he should be classified as a fascist has overtaken American and European academia. Commentators have also tended to read our age through older analytical prisms, with fascism and socialism presented as "the wave of the future," as Edward Luttwak put it in 1994. In March 2019, for instance, Paul Mason posted a comment on his Twitter feed claiming that the Brexit process, recently rattled by another parliamentary rejection, was "now in the hands of the masses." The strange nature of this statement speaks volumes about today's populist moment. Contemporary "populists" on the right, such as Boris Johnson, Matteo Salvini, and Viktor Orbán, might have their followers, sympathizers, likers, and sharers. But one would be hard-pressed to call any of these fandoms "a mass affair." Rather, the 2010s brought forth a new politics of the swarm, with movements headed not by party tribunes, but by what the sociologist Paolo Gerbaudo has called "hyperleaders"—figures whose media presence imparted coherence to a coalition where otherwise there would be none.[10] None of these leaders preside over a society riven by pitched battles and organized class conflict of the kind last seen in the first half of the twentieth century. As Adam Tooze notes, with no world wars the "missing ingredient in the classic fascist equation . . . is social antagonism, a threat, whether imagined or real, to the social and economic status quo."[11] Fascism is here best seen as a civil war waged on the labor movement, itself only a minor presence in the age of the digital swarm. Latin America set a telling precedent here. Where left populists were able to institutionalize and survive their electoral cycles—such as MAS in Bolivia—they did so with the twin preconditions of a commodity boom and clear labor links. Both these commodity and labor factors were lacking in European left-populist cases, compounding the earlier problem of disorganization.[12]

The shift from mass to swarm politics appeared to render obsolete many of the formulae the left had inherited and preserved from the twentieth century. As Dylan Riley already noted in the late 2000s, "the contemporary politics of the advanced-capitalist world bears scant resemblance to that of the interwar period." Back then, "populations organized themselves into mass parties of the left and right," as opposed to "a crisis of politics as a form of human activity," where "it is unlikely that either [Eduard] Bernstein or Lenin can offer lessons directly applicable."[13]

What would a viable alternative to this frame look like? As Riley suggests, a far more telling precedent for our situation can be found in Karl Marx's account of France as the revolutionary wave of 1848 receded. Instead of caving into unrest, Napoleon III gathered an apathetic peasant population and ordered them to quell the revolution. Marx described this French peasantry as a "sack of potatoes" whose "converging interests create no commonality, no national association, and no political organization among them." And since the peasants could not represent themselves, "they had to be represented"— in this case by a king. One-sided notions of representation proved only one aspect of this legacy. Rather than a politics pitting workers against bosses, structured by the capital–labor opposition, Bonaparte's was a politics of debtors and creditors—another shared feature with the 2010s, in which private debts transferred onto public accounts fueled the American and European crises. It was also a politics centered on circulation and taxes, rather than production.

If this is so, rather than to the class wars of the 1930s, we should look back to a much older, primal age of democracy for suitable parallels with our populist age. Once we free our notion of populism from that more recent past, we can properly understand what gave us the current populist moment in the first place. Divergences with the worlds of mass democracy we have left behind will also become visible, and the resulting confusion over the term "populism" will clear up—and so, hopefully, will Paul Mason's trading the streets of Athens for the offices of Whitehall.

1.

WHAT POPULISM?

What is the greatest threat to Western civilization today? In 2011, a journalist put that question to one of Europe's leading officials, the Belgian EU president, Herman Van Rompuy. It was during an obvious moment of crisis for Europe: earlier that year, antiausterity insurrections had broken out in Greece and Spain, while Italy's elected government was being replaced with a band of technocrats. In conversation with the German daily *Frankfurter Allgemeine*, Van Rompuy offered a succinct response: "The greatest danger to the contemporary West," he coolly informed the journalist, "is populism."

To add to the confusion, the label "populism" was embraced a few years later by none other than the leader of the free world, Barack Hussein Obama. Speaking to a group of Canadian journalists in 2016, the outgoing president was asked about Donald Trump's sudden irruption onto the political stage—a figure incessantly portrayed in Western media as an avatar of "populist" politics. Obama, however, took a different view:

I'm not prepared to say that some of the rhetoric that's been popping up is populist. You know, the reason I ran in 2008, and the reason I ran again, and the reason even after I leave this office I will continue to work in some capacity in public office is because I care about people and want to make sure every kid in America has the same opportunities I had . . . Now I suppose that makes me a "populist." Now, somebody else, who has never shown any regard for workers, has never fought on behalf of social justice issues, who has, in fact, worked against economic opportunity for workers, for ordinary people—they don't suddenly become "populist" because they say something controversial in order to win votes. That's not the measure of populism.

Both anecdotes exemplify long-standing differences between the European and American understandings of the term. Still today, Europeans—and, increasingly, American elites—associate the term with the politically odious and risky. In the run-up to the 2018 German election, for example, the p-word was hurled at both the far-left party Die Linke and the far-right formation Alternative for Germany (AfD), while the winning candidate for chancellor, Angela Merkel, styled herself an "antipopulist." In 2021, candidates such as the far-right firebrand Éric Zemmour and Marine Le Pen were both blackened with the label. Meanwhile, the many-headed hydra of populism has also appeared in Austria, Hungary, Italy, Poland, and Spain. As Obama showed, the consensus on the term's meaning is rather less absolute on the American side; even liberal commentators seemed to have few qualms about labeling Bernie Sanders "a progressive populist" during the 2016 election, while many objected to calling Donald Trump a right-wing one.

Obama and Van Rompuy could at least agree on one thing: few words gave a more tantalizing, but also frustratingly vague, indication of their era than the infamous "p-word." The statistics spoke for themselves: from 1970 to 2010, the number of Anglophone publications using the term rose from 300 to more than 800, creeping to over 1,000 in the 2010s. In English, over 500 academic publications appeared on the topic in 2016 alone. The Cambridge Dictionary proclaimed it Word of the Year for 2017, while the *Guardian* ran an extensive series on the concept.

Words always reflect and alter the worlds that produce them, and the uptake of the term marked a deeper structural trend. Globally, movements purporting to speak on behalf of "the people" won majorities, ousted incumbents, attacked courts, even locked up opponents. In this story, "populism" is both an actor and a symptom, the expression of a deep, protracted crisis rolling across democracies of which Europe is but the epicenter. Pablo Iglesias, Donald Trump, Marine Le Pen, Boris Johnson, Nigel Farage, and Beppe Grillo are just some of the many politicians who have qualified for the label.

This increasing popularity regularly prompts an exasperated question: Is it still possible to add anything worthwhile to a mountainous literature on "populism"? Bookshelves bulging with populist "explosions," "menaces," and "threats" tend to suggest a bleaker prospect: the populism industry is nearing overcapacity. "We've reached peak populism," a journalist exclaimed in 2019, lamenting his colleagues' careless use of the word and urging them to find an alternative—or practice a virtuous silence instead.

At this point, the specialists usually divide into two camps. A first group simply believes that we're stuck with the word, for better or worse, and claim that to surgically remove it from our vocabulary would prove too tiresome. The second group demands that we ban the term from our vocabulary altogether. "The worst we can do with words," George Orwell once proclaimed, "is surrender to them." Since the 1980s at least, this camp has been known as the "populist nihilists," while the other is usually put in the "positivist" bracket. Both groups are marked by a certain indifference to the term's history, or the factors that grant the term its contemporary allure.

Must we float between these two poles? Instead of treating "populism" as an entity outside of history, a properly historical approach would allow us to investigate exactly *how* "populism" entered our dictionary and found its way into our brains, books, essays, newspapers, and onto our television screens. This would force questions on nihilists and addicts alike: Why do we so desperately need the word today? And if we do decide to retain it, as the clunky yet indispensable gadget it has become, can it be salvaged?

Trashing Populism

The invasion of the US Capitol on January 6, 2021, might have come as a shock to the public, yet no surprise to an already booming populism industry. On Facebook, political scientists agreed that the authoritarian takeover attempt was "the logical outcome of far-right populism." When someone inquired how Trump's actions and the invasion of the Capitol "had anything to do with populism," the retort was swift: "Trump is a right-wing populist."

Others contemplated even more reckless readings. In their view, January 6 proved that Trump's supporters deserved to be called "fascists," a label even less honorable than "populists." The two interpretations were, of course, a simple matter of degree of severity within the same frame, which looks to precedents in the 1930s to understand today's politics. As disturbing as the events of the Capitol were, however, the differences with historical fascism's distinctive characteristics (mass organization, militarization of society, scientific racism, aggressive foreign policy, etc.) remain glaring. Furthermore, discarding the term "fascism" does not preclude us from criticizing and fighting the political threats of our time—indeed, a lucid understanding of their specificity is likely to make our weapons against them more effective. As the French philosopher Marcel Gauchet recently pointed out, one does not need to brand Marine Le Pen a "fascist" to oppose her politically.[1]

The demands of this frame can often drive analysts into absurd trains of thought. In his best-seller *What Is Populism?*, Jan-Werner Müller boldly argued that since the People's Party of the late nineteenth century in the United States was not anti-pluralist, it should not be considered "populist" at all—even though this was the movement that first claimed the name for itself.[2] This mode of thinking makes about as much sense as a history of communism that disqualifies Marx.

But the media commentary here lies downstream from an altogether different profession. Academia remains the true headquarters of the populism industry. Entire media narratives are based on professorial definitions and analyses; academics are the ones who draw the public's attention to the "problem with populism" and its "undeniable dark side," both in rightist and leftist variants. "Populology" was the word coined by the scholar Federico Tarragoni to brand—and criticize—the common sense created by this intersection between academic and media discourses on populism.[3] Examples abound. On the *Guardian* website, readers are invited to take a quiz to find out "how populist you are," to then be placed in a quadrant chart somewhere among Pablo Iglesias, Evo Morales, Bernie Sanders, Matteo Salvini, Donald Trump, and Viktor Orbán. Populology here turns into a new astrology: much like the personality tests in weeklies, the expert-run quiz brings out your inner populist through innocent questions such as, "Should politicians always listen closely to the problems of the people?" or, "Are the people you disagree with evil?" The *Guardian*'s charts are based on Cas Mudde's definition of populism as a "thin-centered" (based on a minimal set of core principles) ideology: one "that considers society to be ultimately separated into two homogeneous and antagonistic groups, 'the pure people' versus 'the corrupt elite', and which argues that politics should be an expression of the *volonté générale* (general will) of the people."[4]

This minimal criterion lends the definition an air of cool neutrality. The same minimalism, however, also unleashes a fevered paranoia among academics and journalists: suddenly one detects populism *everywhere*. If a belief in politics as the conflict between a virtuous people and a corrupt establishment is enough to brand someone a populist, virtually every modern political actor would appear on the list of suspects.

Like any drug, the journalistic understanding of "populism" both calms and clouds the user's nervous system. Firstly, it leads them to underestimate the real threats besetting Western democracies (nationalism, nativism, cynicism) and glosses them with an unmerited antiestablishment veneer. Le Pen's proposal to throw all the migrants out is no longer "racist" but simply "populist," while Orbán's border guard becomes the popular front. It also allows liberal elites—hardly without blame for the popular resentment that fueled the rise of these so-called populists in the first place—to claim first rank in fighting them. In this sense, it puts a group of arsonists in charge of the firefighters' brigade.

An even graver danger lurks inside the fascist frame, however. As should be clear, the word "populism" logically presupposes the notion of "the people"—the implicit subject of all our capitalist democracies. By proxy, the negative use of the word ends up draping the demos itself in suspicion: *any* popular movement voicing economic, cultural, or political grievances can henceforth be tainted with antidemocratic dispositions. Although almost every modern philosophical tradition places popular sovereignty at the core of democratic principles, citizens are now told that the main danger is the people running against democracy itself, jeopardizing "our freedom."[5] Since Marine Le Pen declares a love for "the people," we must surely grow to hate that entity at all costs. Since Orbán styles himself a "democrat," we must become wary of democracy itself.

Wading through this morass is not only politically exhausting; it also seems pointless in the face of historical inquiry. After all, not all populists have been nationalists and not all nationalists have been populists. Comparative history remains the best detox here: what stands out from the American and Russian experience of populism in the late nineteenth century, or from Corbynism, the Yellow Vests, and the Five Star Movement—to name some of today's populist forces—is certainly not their chauvinist commitment to "the nation." Instead, they are known for their radically democratic claims, seeking to expand the boundaries of what counts as "the people" in the first place. They have often acted as forces of *anti*nationalism, as in the case of Evo Morales redesigning the Bolivian Constitution to turn his country into a "plurinational" one, or Podemos defending a regionalist model for the Spanish state.

"Nationalism" and "fascism" are hardly the most unforgivable of populist sins, however. To opponents, populists are chiefly guilty of engaging in a particularly perverse political style. In this view, populists lean into an opportunistic, cynical, manipulative *way* of doing politics. Thus "populism" becomes an accusation of "demagoguery," without ever openly stating it. This slippage—by definition, two concepts can never be perfect synonyms—allows liberal elites, journalists, academics, and politicians alike to blame the individual actions of agents and avoid analysis of the deeper preconditions of populism's rise, along with any admission of their own responsibility. Scary portraits of Steve Bannon, Donald Trump's "black star," take the place of serious sociology.[6] The rise of populism, in this view, is the regrettable result of dangerous demagogues exploiting the natural frustrations generated by globalization.

In such a climate, it is hardly surprising that the radical right has warmed to the term. Nationalists and nativists—often men of property themselves—get generously rebranded as defenders of the common man against capitalist elites. Conversely, public debate tends to conflate populism and reactionary politics, the negative connotations of the latter polluting the former. Any form of popular mobilization is now devalued by the specters of bigotry and authoritarianism. Much like the concept of totalitarianism during the Cold War, the notion of populism can be used to *reduce* rather than expand our political options, collapsing any possible challenge to the current order into a disaster waiting to happen.[7] Like its predecessor, it simply folds together the two ends of the political spectrum as somehow equally reprehensible, since both exploit the frustrations of the people for their own ends; Bernie, Le Pen, Orbán, and Iglesias all wind up grouped in the same camp.

Before us lies the following puzzle: a term once used to refer to progressive, multiracial movements aiming to strengthen democracy and reduce social inequalities is now used to designate a *threat* to democracy. At the heart of this paradox, we find a growing schism between two of the central concepts of modernity, "people" and "democracy," now openly cast as opposites—as seen in book titles such as *The People vs. Democracy*, or *Against Democracy*. How did we get here?

Historicizing Populism

Across the last two centuries, the trajectory of the Anglophone word "populism" looks something like what is outlined below.

For nearly the whole first half, the line stays perfectly flat. A gentle upward curve around 1890 builds into a hill, which slopes upward for about five years and then stabilizes downward, until about 1940. From 1955 onwards, things begin to change: the line turns into a steep graph, which rises to a peak around 1960. By 2000, we see a momentary slowdown, although previous levels are in no way diminished, while by 2016 (a well-known populist *annus horribilis*) the line has begun a stiff run upward again.

"Only concepts without histories can be defined," Friedrich Nietzsche once said, and the same inevitably holds for populism, a word which traversed countless debates before it found its current definition. This genealogy is also rife with awkward surprises. Rather than with Greek orators, Roman senators, or Nazi stormtroopers, the journey of the word "populism" begins in a small town in the Midwest. In June 1891, a group of rebellious farmers gathered in the city of Omaha, Nebraska, to kick-start a movement that would run in elections the following year, when the group would morph into a fully fledged party— the People's Party. This party was based on a vast and intricate network of Farmers' Alliances and producer cooperatives. Its radical farmers faced a minor but tricky conundrum when on the campaign trail. Everyone knew what to call a member of the Democratic or Republican Party; but what was a short and snappy term for a member of the People's Party?

In 1892, they found their solution and proposed the term "Populist"—thereby launching the career of our now 130-year-old concept as well as one of the most formidable social movements in American history. From the 1870s to the 1900s, white and black Populists built movements which stitched together a coalition of workers and farmers, represented by organizations such as the Farmers' Alliance, the Grange, the Colored Farmers' Alliance, and the 1891 People's Party. Its Omaha Platform (1892) called for the nationalization of the American railroad system, the centralization of federal monetary policy, and the burial of rivalries left over from the American Civil War. As the platform declared:

> We meet in the midst of a nation brought to the verge of moral, political, and material ruin. Corruption dominates the ballot-box, the Legislatures, the Congress, and touches even the ermine of the bench . . . The fruits of the toil of millions are boldly stolen to build up colossal fortunes for a few, unprecedented in the history of mankind; and the possessors of those, in turn, despise the republic and endanger liberty. From the same prolific womb of governmental injustice we breed the two great classes—tramps and millionaires.[8]

For a period in the early 1890s, American history seemed to be moving in a Populist direction. The "Pops'" presidential candidate, James B. Weaver, achieved a respectable 14 percent in the 1892 presidential election; in 1894, the party went on to capture a sizable number of seats in Western and Southern states. The Eastern bourgeoisie grew terrified of this agrarian revolt, while Midwestern capitalists rallied to crush it. In his private diaries, for instance, Theodore Roosevelt looked forward to Populists being "put up against the wall and shot," since their campaign was nothing less "than an appeal to the torch."[9]

Antipopulist tactics were not particularly subtle, in any region. In the 1896 election, Eastern banks dispatched representatives into Midwestern towns to warn farmers that their homes would be foreclosed upon if they dared to elect any Populist lawmakers. It was in Southern states, however, that Populists faced their mightiest opposition. Efforts to unite black and white tenant farmers against the local landlord-merchant alliance were met with brutal repression, aided by elites' stranglehold over Southern commodity markets. Dixiecrats fought off the Populist threat with physical intimidation, alcoholic bribes, and stuffed ballot boxes.

In desperation, Populists began to search for allies within established American parties. In 1896, the Democratic Party co-opted the Populist platform by nominating William Jennings Bryan, a proponent of "free silver" (a moderately inflationary policy), for president. After bitter intra-party debate, the Populists decided to put Bryan's name on their own ticket, rather than field a candidate against him. It proved a fateful decision. After Bryan's loss to the Republican William McKinley, the party disintegrated. Most of its cadre would go on to join other political outfits, such as Eugene V. Debs's American Socialist Party, or the vibrant Farmer–Labor coalitions of the 1920s.

For Americans, "populism" still evokes memories of masses on the move, democratic renewal, or torrents of abuse hurled at elites. In the 1980s, the writer Saul Bellow could reminisce about his New Deal years in the 1930s as a "populist" heyday, while liberal writers more recently styled Bernie's campaign for president a "populist" insurgency.[10]

The term also took a while to cross the pond. In the 1930s, *populisme* began popping up in France; in the 1950s, it first appeared in Spanish, Czech, and German. The writer Vladimir Nabokov was commissioned to write something on a French "populist manifesto" in 1933. The philosopher Jean-Paul Sartre printed articles on "populism" in his magazine, *Les Temps Modernes*, in the 1950s. On the whole, however, Europeans saw the word as something foreign—a word with "arcane meanings not readily apparent to the ordinary reader," as one social scientist confessed in the 1950s.[11]

How did the American product finally find its way to European markets? As usual, academics turned out to be the most capable smugglers. In the 1970s and 1980s a burgeoning field of far-right studies took up the term, which subsequently migrated to Europe's media pages. Most researchers in this field drew on the work of the historian Richard Hofstadter, who had portrayed American populism as "proto-fascist" in the 1950s. One of the most influential of these academics was the French political scientist Pierre-André Taguieff, who in 1984 labeled the rising National Front as "national-populist," rather than the old and outworn "fascist." By the early 1990s, French academia and media were rife with discussions of "*le populisme*." In 1994, the Front's leader Jean-Marie Le Pen eagerly claimed the term for himself, finding it less tainted than the fascist label—a stigma the party was now anxious to cast off. "If it stands for 'speaking for the people'," Le Pen quipped to a journalist, "then I certainly am a populist."[12]

The French were not alone in experiencing this migration. In the same years as Taguieff, British political scientist Stuart Hall began to draft analyses on Thatcher's Conservative party as "authoritarian populist." To Hall, this definition captured Thatcher's attempt to unite wealthier white-collar workers, small business owners, and London's high finance in a single pro-market coalition.[13] By the end of the 1990s the word "populism" was ubiquitous, from French newspapers to MTV news anchors, reflexively applied to the Paris multimillionaire Bernard Tapie, the Italian television star Silvio Berlusconi, or the British prime minister Tony Blair, who beatified the late Princess Diana as "the people's princess." Like a drug, "populism" had flooded European markets—and the specialists were hooked.

The post-2008 era turbocharged this addiction. Suddenly, academics rushed to the populism industry while newspaper editors churned out op-eds. The gap between what populism now stood for and what it once meant was clear. To Europeans the radical farmers still hovered somewhere in the background, but only as distant ancestors. (The Russians, however, remain keenly aware of this discrepancy and use different words for their own "populist" movements: the original *narodnichestvo* of the late nineteenth century, and the current *popoulizmo*, here denoting a coarser form of demagoguery.)

Until recently, Americans appeared immune to this trend. Tied to their original nineteenth-century experience, US commentators found it difficult to apply the word "populist" to the species of politician emerging in Europe. In the 1960s, Civil Rights leaders such as Martin Luther King and Bayard Rustin could still look back on the original populism as a noteworthy chapter in the people's history of the United States. More concretely, King referenced the original Populists' biracial efforts in speeches at the 1965 Selma march. Figures such as Ross Perot, Ronald Reagan, or Michael Dukakis might have been disparaged with the epithet in the 1990s. Beyond the Washington bubble, however, "populism" had not lost its radical luster.

The turbulent 2010s finally put an end to this exceptionalism. After Trump stormed into the White House, American commentators began reaching for analytical lifelines. From what hellish dimension had this creature sprung? Surely America had always had its own indigenous demons? Scouring the historical record, and then checking in with what their European counterparts were up to, it became clear what was to blame. Trump was a "populist," or "a populist demagogue." And in European taxonomy, the word lacked the left-wing associations it had on the other side of the Atlantic.

The results were often hard to decipher. "Populism now stands for 'I don't know what it is, but I was asked to talk about it'," the Hungarian critic Gáspár Tamás noted in 2017, poking fun at the large consultancy industry which had grown around the term.[14] In his view, many political scientists embarked on research projects on populism simply in hopes of getting a gig: politicians concerned about how the "populist menace" might affect their home countries (or careers) frequently hired such specialists to inform them. Since the terms of the research are set in advance, its results are painfully predictable, with some minor variations as to whether the politician in question should engage with the toxic "populists" or shun them.

Still, "populism" refuses to die and remains a highly malleable concept. With no suitable alternatives, it is—for most of those who deploy it—simply a word groping for an analysis. Yet our enduring attraction to the term needs explaining. Rather as in the parable of the boy pointing at the moon, we need to look at both the finger *and* the moon: although the latter might forever remain shrouded behind the clouds, the fact that the boy felt the need to point at it remains interesting enough. *Something* is out there. In the end, the appeal of the term "populism" indicates a hidden yet powerful dynamic in our current democratic crisis. As European and American parties lost members, and techno-crats seized control of the state, the word signaled a widely misunderstood but nonetheless real shift in how Atlantic democracies themselves functioned.

In this light, using "populism" should never be the *end* of a conversation. Rather, it confronts users with a series of questions from which a frank discussion of the last thirty years of Western politics can finally begin. From the small Midwestern farmers who first claimed the word in the late nineteenth century, to the European television pundits who brandished it in the 1990s, "populism" expresses an uncomfortable truth about how our European and American democracies have changed—indirectly expressed in *how* we talk about politics. "You might not be interested in the war," Leon Trotsky said to young communists lamenting the start of the 1914 mobilization, "but the war *is* interested in you." Similarly, we might not be interested in the word "populism"; ultimately, however, the word remains all too interested in us.

Thickening Populism

The populist and socialist traditions have always competed to offer their own response to the same substantial dilemma of the left: With what base and what ideology can it grow its majority? Whereas socialism crowns the industrial working class as the sovereign around which all others must coalesce (peasantry, middle class), the populist approach has always been different.

Almost by default, populist movements traverse class divides. Their coalition typically encompasses a variety of social groups from the lower to the middle classes, from the urban to the suburban and rural. Most importantly, in populist politics, none of these groups enjoys a privileged role as the political actor par excellence. Rather than forging a social bloc *around* a class—which presupposes the existence of an acute class consciousness of itself and its historical mission—populism articulates a coalition *across* classes. As a result, populism's political subject is both broader and vaguer than socialism's proletariat: populism's people is an abstract subject that all too easily merges with the subject of democracy. No wonder democracy is the true cornerstone of populism's ideology. From the farmers to the radical professors in Madrid's universities, populists have always been more interested in expanding and radicalizing the scope of democratic principles than in seizing the means of production. They have always pushed for the inclusion of the popular sectors by granting them equal civil, political, social, and economic rights and fostering their participation through assemblies, cooperatives, and, in today's politics, digital forms of direct democracy. Capitalism and representative democracy were never populism's prime adversaries; oligarchic corruption always was. Populism always remained uneasy about setting up a politics around the capital–labor matrix, and instead preferred oppositions between debtors and creditors, elites and peoples.

Populism thus responded to the first dilemma of the modern left—working or middle class?—by unashamedly broadening its base. This implied the simplification of its ideological content and the complexification of its form, in terms of both rhetoric and organization. As a linguist would put it, populism gains in *extension* what it loses in *intension*: its lack of social specificity broadens the range of its application. This abstract nature, so to speak, of populist politics was perfectly captured by Ernesto Laclau in his *On Populist Reason*. In Laclau's view, populism is the process by which a leader unifies popular demands based on their opposition to a common enemy, thereby constructing a "people" against a power bloc.

This formalism also comes with risks, however. If populism refers *only* to the process by which demands are linked together and has no sociological or ideological content of its own, it can take countless forms. Once more we are left with Podemos and Vox, Mélenchon and Le Pen, Bernie and Trump, as two sides of the same coin. Would we ever say that the difference between

Lenin and Mussolini was only a distinction of secondary impor-
tance compared to their formal similarities? "Populism," as
vague as it might seem, still grows out of the same soil and
is faced with the same challenge as socialism: how to build a
coherent form of emancipatory politics based on heterogeneous social forces.

A majoritarian social bloc does not arise *ex nihilo*. Without
being overdetermined by the relations of production, it is
not completely independent of them either. Hence the political economy of populism: the harder it is to reduce political
conflict to a binary opposition between capital and labor in the
manufacturing sector, the less the industrial working class can
regard itself as the key political subject for social transformation—and the more tempting a populist approach will be for
the left. In the 2010s as in the late nineteenth or mid-twentieth
centuries, populism picked up social democracy's slack in situations of extreme social fragmentation and disorganization.
In terms of policies, too, it worked as a functional equivalent
of social democracy's reformist agenda, expanding the scope
of civil and political rights while laying the foundations for
future welfare states.

In that regard, the context in which Laclau built his theory
of populism is noteworthy. While he took inspiration from the
Peronist regime in his home country, his primary interven-
tions took place in the Marxist debates of the late 1980s, when
deindustrialization and the rise of new struggles including civil
rights, feminism, and environmentalism were redefining the
terms of the substantial dilemma that had always haunted the
left. As Perry Anderson has noted, his work thereby strangely

"anticipated developments in Europe thirty years later, when globalization had shrunk and divided the working class, leaving a much more fragmented social landscape, and a multiplication of movements, left and right, contesting the established order in the name of the people."[15] For the left, the return of the populist temptation went hand in hand with the shattering of the original coalition on which social democracy had built its successes.

In many ways, the debates of the 2010s echoed this turbulence. Populist breakthroughs usually happen when a spark—economic recession, fiscal reform, or modernization/globalization—first ignites a *crisis of representation*. Then a broad swath of the society comes to see democracy as having been perverted by an oligarchic minority's plundering of public resources. Populism rides in as the white knight of "real democracy," either to defend it against the hijack of its existing structures (the oligopolistic takeover of the United States in the late nineteenth century, the technocratic handling of the eurozone crisis in the aftermath of 2008) or to force its advent against the bottlenecks of pre-democratic societies (Tsarist Russia, Latin American landlordism). Through this lens we can see a common thread between the populist moments of past and present. From the People's Party to the Five Star Movement, the populist moments erupt in situations where a social democratic option was either unavailable or discredited, the channels of democratic mediation were clogged, and the main social groups of a popular coalition were relatively fragmented and isolated, and so crying out for unification.

Populism can never be a "pure" phenomenon, however. The protagonists of this book have all, to some extent, created hybrid forms of politics between the social democratic, communist, and populist traditions. All of them, however, have gone through at least one specific *moment* in their development in which the populist approach was dominant. All of them were forced to construct "the people" as a political subject and find a charismatic leader to embody their hopes, dreams and demands; all of them fed on the strong antagonism between this popular subject and a power bloc; all of them called for the expansion of rights and economic redistribution to popular sectors; all of them sought mass participation across classes; and, finally, all of them rose up during moments of democratic crises. To accomplish its populist turn, the left wore different organizational clothes, from brand-new political formations (Podemos) to radical innovations within pre-existing marginal parties (Syriza, La France insoumise), to strategies aiming at conquering intra-party leadership within established mainstream parties (Corbyn, Sanders).

The populist turn of the 2010s was no perfect replica of its Russian, US, and Latin American predecessors. Rather, four decades of declining turnout, plummeting party membership, discredited ideologies, and a generally atomized society had considerably changed the coordinates of political activity. Western democracies had endured a slow but steady process of disintermediation: the bodies (parties, unions, churches, clubs, etc.) that used to link the citizens to society declined everywhere, thereby causing the extreme fragmentation and disorganization of the social groups to which the left used to appeal. These developments, coupled with the increasing digitalization of politics, have added considerable complexity to the century-old substantial dilemma. Aggregating disparate interests is a totally different game these days: rather than the 1890s or the 1930s, today's social landscape looks more like 1848's "sack of potatoes."

Populism is, then, simply one of the various species inhabiting this new political "ecosystem" of disorganized democracy—alongside the new radical right and the liberal technocrats. It is particularly skilled at adapting itself to the new setting: its vast experience in articulating demands and its strong criticism of the current state of democracy perfectly match the spirit of our time. Organizationally, however, contemporary populism hardly resembles its historical precedents, with their dense networks of cooperatives, unions, and popular committees. To survive in the new environment, the populist left has adopted a light and digital form of organization. Contrary to an all-too-common view, however, the antiestablishment rhetoric, the strong leadership, the plebiscitarian modes of decision, the direct channels of communication and the weak party structures are not specific to populist actors. Rather, they characterize *any* new actor eager to thrive in our present environment—thus fostering the confusion in public debate, where Salvini, Macron, and Iglesias are often thrown together for this very reason. "Men resemble their times more than they do their fathers," as the Arab proverb has it.[16] Much like the late nineteenth-century Populists should be put in their post–Civil War context, the fact that Bernie and Trump are two of the protagonists of the new era—just as Lenin and Mussolini were once the epitomes of mass politics—does not mean they should be considered as a single political phenomenon.

Herman Van Rompuy was right, in at least one unexpected sense: a populist moment was taking place in the 2010s. He was insightful enough to see it from the outset. It should now be clearer, however, what he meant by the term. Based on the baneful connotations the p-word had accumulated throughout its turbulent history—a mix of demagoguery, illiberalism, and irrationality—he aimed to discredit the antiausterity movements that were flourishing all over the West, by depicting them as a threat to liberal democracy.

Rehabilitation through history, however, gives us a different story: democracy is, in fact, at the core of populist claims. The flower of populism only blossoms when there is a perceived crisis of representation. Van Rompuy, after all, was speaking in a specific capacity, as the informal leader of a group of countries that were set to impose rigid austerity on reluctant populations, while bypassing the most elementary forms of democratic control. A few years later, Jean-Claude Juncker would be even more explicit, claiming that "there can be no democratic choice against the European Treaties." The ease with which powerful European figures were dismissing democracy itself spoke volumes. At the same time, the traditional vehicles of social struggle—center-left parties and trade unions—were now largely incapable of channeling popular discontent as they had in the past. This was due to the heterogeneity of the expressions of discontent as much as the discrediting of the old party vehicles. The democratic vacuum, in turn, resulted from both short-term dynamics and long-term tendencies: while its origins lay in the ramshackle elite management of the 2008 crisis, their blunders only accelerated the decline of party democracy that had already been underway for decades.

2.

WHY POPULISM?

He'd picked a catchy title, to say the least. Paul Mason's *Why It's Kicking Off Everywhere* (2012) was a reflection on the global turmoil he'd witnessed firsthand as a journalist, before he began his cheerleading for Syriza, Corbyn, and other left-populist figures. After decades of political quietude punctuated by short intervals of activity, 2011 indeed proved an unusually bumpy year for Western elites. Starting with the Arab Spring a few months before, protests spread like wildfire and went global, reaching even the most iconic temple of contemporary capitalism via the Occupy Wall Street movement. In the meantime, Madrid and Athens had seen the Puerta del Sol and Syntagma Square taken over by thousands of citizens protesting the austerity measures implemented by their governments. After the long freeze of the 2000s, mass mobilization was seemingly back from the dead. People had returned to the streets—or, more precisely, the squares—in such numbers that *Time* magazine nominated "The Protester" as Person of the Year.

There was something new about the way these social movements arose—the what, the where, the who, and the how. This upheaval did not look much like the classic demonstrations staged by the left over the past decades: sectorial and self-referential, led by declining labor organizations or vanguardist students' movements. Rather, these movements happened in quick succession and went far beyond the usual suspects of the left. They mobilized across economic sectors and classes, largely outside established party organizations, and deployed a specific inventory of symbols. The financial crisis and its aftermath had profoundly changed the terms of the original dilemma of substance.

That the "movements of the squares" broke out across such a narrow time frame also proved revealing. It showed that contagion across nations and continents was no longer restricted to financial risks—or to viruses—but could also occur in the realm of social mobilization, from which the internet had considerably removed barriers of space and time. Most importantly, it implied that *something was going on*. It is one thing to witness a social uprising in a specific national context; it is quite another to observe the breaking of a wave of mass protests all around the globe at nearly the same time. Such synchronicity points to deeper factors: the square movements indicated that one type of capitalism in its neoliberal phase was going through a deep and protracted crisis. As we shall see later in this chapter, the specific nature of that crisis—at least in its transatlantic expression, leaving aside the aspects related to authoritarianism in Egypt and Tunisia—was created by the intersection of two major events: the catastrophic management of the 2008 economic crisis, and the decline of democratic institutions. One was short-term and gave the square movements most of their vocabulary, which would later be taken up by left-populist formations. The second factor, having slowly incubated over past decades marked by the demise of traditional political parties, would determine the specific form of organization endorsed by populist insurgents. It had added a dilemma of form to the dilemma of substance, thus multiplying the difficulty of the latter.

The squares' strength and successes had different roots, depending on their ability to build a coalition between three demographic segments that did not usually march together.[1] First, the "lost generation," a young and highly educated part of the population, harshly affected by the crisis, was flocking to the squares. In the US, these "connected outsiders" were known as the new grad class, the students buckling under the burden of debt. Their European cousins, the Erasmus generation depicted in the mid-2000s film *L'auberge espagnole*, had benefited from free movement within the EU, only to find themselves broke after their studies ended.

Disproportionately unemployed—or forced into a low-wage service sector—the euro-generation was generally offered an unattractive choice between two options: living with their parents well into their thirties, or migrating in search of decent jobs. In Italy, Spain, and Greece, this generational divide had become one of the most sensitive issues, offering a new rallying tool for political parties. Indeed, progressive and conservative actors alike increasingly tended to reframe social antagonism along those lines. Podemos, for instance, tried to pinpoint (youth) *emigration*, rather than immigration, as the main problem faced by Spanish society. The Italian elites, in

contrast, became infamous for stigmatizing the lost generation—which anyway does not vote for them—and branding
it as the lazy author of its own fate.[2]

The second group present on the squares was an increasingly "squeezed middle class." Back in the 1990s, the middle
class was the group that most indirectly sustained the Third
Way turn of the left—they were, in fact, its prime beneficiaries. Working for the most part in the public and service
sectors, this social group was hit hard by both the 2008 crisis
and the austerity plans that followed only to finally, after
two decades, begin to feel the negative effects of neoliberal
reforms. This newly impoverished group coalesced with
the one it was now afraid of becoming: the "new poor."
Composed of the long-term unemployed, the homeless, and
the new "working poor," this tag-along part of the coalition
was also, historically, the most difficult to mobilize—the
trade unions had repeatedly failed to rally them since the
1970s, for instance.

But it was the third group whose relative absence from the
squares would soon become deeply consequential—the surviving industrial working class. This group was torn between
its typical exit, voice, and loyalty strategies: while its most
passive components stubbornly refused to vote or opted for
the far right, the others remained staunchly loyal to the social
democrats. Here was a weakness that would become a perva-
sive feature of the populist left and a thorn in its side. The
protesters tended to approach traditional trade unions with a
mix of suspicion and hostility—as in Spain and Greece, where
they were slammed for their collusion with discredited social

democratic parties—or an attitude of stepmotherly compliance, as in Corbynism.

The rhetoric deployed by the squares movements was also strikingly contemporaneous. Their slogans, demands, and chants bore only a faint resemblance to those of the historical labor movement. Instead, they harked back to those of the antiglobalization mobilizations that flourished in the late 1990s and early 2000s. All of these had shared a clear labor component, of course, mainly through the American Federation of Labor's (AFL-CIO) hostility to international trade deals. Yet the new protesters' primary backing did not originate within the classical labor movement, either. With no powerful institution like the labor movement to call upon, leftists were forced to take the battle to the electoral arena, thereby launching the true left-populist gamble. Prior to this, many observers had already identified a populist component in the square movements, expressed in mottoes such as "We are the 99 percent," "They do not represent us," or "They call it democracy and it is not." Their main targets were not capitalists and multinational corporations per se. Instead they attacked the unholy alliance between economic and political elites—the "caste."

This marked a significant divergence from older socialist approaches. Rather than relying upon the old industrial working class, these new populists sought to construct a broad and inclusive popular subject, capable of reclaiming democratic institutions in the name of "the many not the few." To a certain extent, this was a pragmatic way to deal with their extreme heterogeneity. As Ernesto Laclau points out, the construction of any broad popular coalition rests upon the identification of a common enemy and the use of symbols that tend toward ambiguity, so as to represent all the coalition's components. This language, however, was more than a mere strategic tool: as we shall see later in this chapter, it also reflected a specific (populist) imaginary related to the dynamics of the crisis itself.

One year later, however, the energy had dissipated. The movements of the squares gradually faded away without winning any substantial policy gains. In Spain and Greece, it was the conservative parties which primarily benefited from the fall of incumbent social democratic governments. Mariano Rajoy in December 2011, then Antonis Samaras six months later, took office ready and willing to tighten the austerity noose even more. Financial cuts were presented as an act of penance for a society that had lived beyond its means. We were reaping what we had sown. At this point, the elites were still in a state of total hubris. Faced with movements they thought innocuous, they unleashed their contempt for the rabble without restraint. In Italy, Beppe Grillo's notion to compete for the presidency of the Democratic Party (PD)—after having surfed the wave of antipolitics for years—was welcomed with irony. The PD leader sneered in 2009 that Grillo should "set up a party and stand in elections," adding that "we would see how many votes he gets." Karma took its revenge: less than ten years later, the Five Star Movement was the largest individual party in Italy, with a clear majority of seats in parliament. In Spain, too, the Popular Party in power felt confident enough to urge the heirs of the Indignados's 15-M to "pursue their objectives through votes, rather than with placards alone."

Several months later, ruling groups would have their bluff called. In Greece, a radical left coalition, Syriza, overtook the collapsing social democratic party and became the second largest political force in the country during the 2012 national election. In Spain, Podemos ("We Can"), a new political formation, gestated in 2012 and 2013 in the classrooms of Madrid's Complutense University, officially turned into a political party in March 2014, with the explicit goal of carrying the Indignados's legacy into the electoral arena. It scored a surprising 8 percent in the 2014 European elections and enjoyed steady growth until the year 2016. A few years later, other political forces would spring up across Western countries: the Bernie Sanders campaign would energize the American left, Jeremy Corbyn would take over the Labour Party, and Jean-Luc Mélenchon would almost make it to the second round of the French presidential election with his new political platform, La France insoumise.

These new electoral challengers looked both backward and forward. On the one hand, they veered away from their most "horizontal" tendencies, as they were explicitly on a quest for institutional power. On the other, they broadly shared the same sociological and linguistic features. Like the movements from which they emerged, their political grammar was articulated around the people, rather than the working class. There was more to it, however. These new political actors hardly looked like the classic form of organizations we were used to seeing on the left. They were actively *departing* from the mass party model and its dense structures. They had no large memberships and few roots in civil society, nor were there hives of cadres busy on the long, painstaking work of party-building. Instead, these parties were built quickly, revolving primarily around a charismatic leader and the inventive use of new media. In so doing they were adapting to the contemporary environment, where political predators succeed only insofar as they manage to mobilize large numbers of disaffiliated, individuals as quickly as possible. Once again, they were a new kind of political species in a changing ecosystem.

So where did this massive wave of mobilization and the ensuing populist turn come from? If initial claims of injustice were a reaction to the mismanagement of the economic crisis, the organizations that arose in response reflected and even mimicked the rampant hollowing out of civil society over the past several decades. The 2008 crash and the 2010–13 convulsions of the euro brutally accelerated an underlying trend: the slow erosion of party democracy. Hence, the short history of content and the long history of narrated below.

Managing the Crisis

Crises rarely come with an instruction manual. They are moments of daunting ambiguity for both decision-makers and citizens: it is extremely difficult to predict the policy responses they will trigger, as well as the kinds of protest they will unleash. When the stock market unexpectedly collapsed in 2008, nobody guessed that it would spur the outbreak of a *populist moment* across the Western world. Things could have unfolded entirely differently. The crisis could have caused a paradigm shift among political elites, turning them away from neoliberal economics and generating a new consensus around neo-Keynesian solutions (regulation of financial activity, public investment, expansionary monetary policy, etc.). Most academic commentators were expecting exactly such a shift, and they were quite puzzled by the "strange non-death of neoliberalism."[3] It could have provoked expressions of authoritarian, nationalist, and xenophobic sentiment among the population—and, to a certain extent, it did. It could have regenerated the labor movement and revived its political organizations—and in some places, like Portugal, it also did. Given the extreme fragmentation and atomization of the left's social base, however, the main result was quite different: it gave rise to a wave of protests firmly expressed in the language of democracy, that would later serve as an inspiration for new political contenders such as Bernie Sanders, Pablo Iglesias, Alexis Tsipras, Jeremy Corbyn, and Jean-Luc Mélenchon. This could hardly be the automatic result of *any* economic crisis. It rather resulted from the unlikely intertwining of three factors: the specific nature of the crisis, its management by the political elites, and the perceived lack of alternatives. In Europe, moreover, the latter two factors were even further accentuated by the structure of the euro area and reigning policy orthodoxy.

Credit Crash

The populist "moment" of the left in the 2010s is a story of disorganization in several regards. In parallel to the demise of political forms of mediation—to which we shall return in the second part of this chapter—there was another kind of disintermediation at play in the US financial sector. Since the

1980s, capitalism had undergone massive changes: the disaggregation of the party and of the state went hand in hand with the decomposition of the classically integrated industrial firm. In the US, the weight of the financial sector within the economy skyrocketed: in the sixty years since the 1950s, it increased from 2.3 to 7.7 percent of American GDP, and its share of the total profit in the US economy doubled between the 1980s and the 2000s to reach 40 percent. This was not a purely "natural" evolution of capitalist preferences, however, but driven by legislation designed to deregulate financial activities. Crucial to this was, for instance, the Gramm-Leach-Bliley Financial Services Modernization Act (1999) that abolished the separation between commercial and investment banking that had existed since the Glass-Steagall Act, adopted in 1933 as a response to the 1929 Wall Street crash. Together with other blunt deregulation measures, it facilitated the access to credit for households and edged out the banks from their central position as intermediary bodies for loans: between the 1980s and the 2000s, their share in the total amount of financial assets plummeted from 50 to 25 percent. It was then increasingly easy for anyone to borrow from the proliferation of uncontrolled financial institutions. In parallel, the welfare societies were giving way to a more individualistic social contract: asset citizenship.

This model, which relied on private debt to maintain growth, had originally been designed as a response to the shocks of the 1970s and 1980s. With the United States and the UK's help, it soon conquered other Western countries. As wages stagnated, productivity fell and inequalities worsened, the old engines of growth were swapped out for easy access to credit. People were earning less (in relative terms) but could borrow more.[4] Money was cheap. It came mainly from emerging countries, whose commercial surpluses ensured large capital inflows to advanced countries. Western governments, by means of this cheap money, were "buying time":[5] they borrowed from expected future profits in order to meet the demands of rising living standards. The new model thus bought social peace—but, as we soon learned, at a steep price.

The rest of the story is well-known. Financial deregulation fueled crash conditions: financial innovation, risk dilution over the chain of shareholders, and a general tendency to underestimate the risks involved. Financial institutions were eager to grant extremely risky mortgage loans to low-income households, which were then merged with other, stronger products to sell them as composite, supposedly "secured" assets (known as collateralized debt obligations). When the housing bubble burst, it dragged down several of the biggest US financial players and unleashed a chain reaction in the rest of the world through tightly connected global financial markets.

This model relied upon selling a fantasy to the public, just as any form of capitalist dominance does. In 1945, to encourage Italian workers to go work 4,000 feet underground in Belgium, to dig the massive quantities of coal that Northern Italian industries needed, government ads depicted Belgian miners rolling cigarettes in banknotes.[6] To convince low-income American households to take on a mortgage, it was necessary to persuade them that they could, in fact, own their house and fulfil the American dream—even if their paycheck said otherwise.

The Bush administration consequently promoted the model of "the ownership society," of which the cornerstones were personal responsibility, economic liberty, and asset holding. At the other end of the financial chain, the seemingly endless rise of asset value and the huge profit opportunities for creditors diffused the idea that capitalism, owing to financial innovation, had finally solved the problem of its cyclical crises. "No bust, only boom" was the new motto: a promise of uninterrupted growth and self-actualization through consumption and private ownership. In the south of Europe, the dreams fed by Northern money acquired an even more illustrious sheen: "modernity" and "democracy" themselves. The crisis was therefore not restricted to the growth model: it also involved the vanishing of the powerful imaginary that accompanied it. When bankers turned against the very households to which they'd granted mortgage loans, and when the government used public money to rescue institutions that were judged "too big to fail," people did get poorer. But they also felt betrayed by the economic and political elites responsible for the situation. Such a sentiment would resurface in the slogans of the Occupy movement. In the European Union, resentment would be even stronger, thanks to the harsh route of austerity taken by national governments.

The Euro Cage

The credit haze was as global as the growth model it was latched onto. The dream of generalized home ownership was not restricted to the United States: on the eve of the crisis in

Spain, for instance, the construction sector accounted for 14 percent of total employment and 16 percent of GDP. For years, it had been the main driver of Iberian growth, with the Irish situation much the same. Between 2004 and 2007, 5 million mortgage loans had been granted in Spain.[7] If the United States was the "consumer of last resort" of the production coming from developing countries, the cheap money sustaining the economic miracles of Spain and the "Celtic tiger" had another name: German profits. Spain's entry into the common currency area provoked massive capital inflows from countries running a surplus and a spectacular decline in interest rates, effectively inciting people to borrow. The 2000s Spanish growth was thus somewhat artificial or "unhealthy"—José Luis Zapatero, Spain's prime minister at the time, would later explain the crisis by comparing the Spanish economy to a body "putting on weight through fat rather than muscle."[8] The euro, in this picture, was supposed to be the dose of steroids.

Both Northern and Southern elites were quick to sell the crisis as one of "sovereign debt." This was allegedly caused by the profligacy of specific states offensively grouped under the "PIIGS" label (Portugal, Ireland, Italy, Greece, Spain). For countries like Ireland and Spain, the diagnosis was blatantly erroneous. In 2007, Spain's net debt-to-GDP ratio was 26 percent, which made it one of the "best in class" among European countries. Private debt had become public only later, through different mechanisms. First, the public finances deteriorated when the government had to rescue the small regional saving banks (*cajas de ahorro*) that were severely vulnerable to the bursting of the real-estate bubble. Second, the economic recession itself had an automatic impact on public accounts by lowering tax revenues and increasing welfare expenses. Third, the initial (timid) recovery plan financed by the socialist government accentuated the deficit. As a result, Spanish public finances endured a spectacular deterioration. The country's total public and private external debt, the figure that really matters in determining a country's solvency, had reached 170 percent of GDP by the end of 2012, making it particularly vulnerable to speculation.[9] Looking only at the Spanish (and Irish) case, the focus on state profligacy sounded whimsical.

The cases of Greece, Italy, and Portugal were different insofar as they *did* retain high levels of public debt prior to the crisis, combined with an auxiliary set of macro-economic weaknesses. These included entrenched corruption, weak tax capacity, and fiscal opacity in Greece, and low growth, an aging population, and low productivity in Italy and Portugal. Even there, however, public debt was not regarded as an intractable problem in the 2000s—on the contrary, the adoption of the euro made borrowing costs fall sharply. Yet it suddenly *became* one from the investors' perspective in a context of global panic. Faced with very different national settings, however, it should have been clear to European decision-makers that there was no one-size-fits-all solution available. So how did austerity suddenly become a magic wand for European politicians?

Any country experiencing this turbulence has several options, depending on its diagnosis. Among these, expansionary monetary policy and public spending to sustain internal demand and boost exports had stood out as levers of a Keynesian economic policy. Austerity was premised on the opposite idea—focusing on budget balancing, which, in times of economic recession and shrinking tax revenues for the state, must be achieved through spending cuts. The austerity cure is often worse than the disease, however, as most of the time it exacerbates the downturn, further shrinking the government's resources while incentivizing new cuts to rebalance its budget.[10]

But when it came to the euro crisis, there hardly was much of a choice matrix for government leaders. As hinted above, entry into the eurozone had facilitated capital transfers from one country to another, and rapid yet heavily debt-dependent growth in "peripheral" countries. Yet there was another side to the common coin: it functioned as a disciplinary instrument on national governments. The constraint was both ideological and material. Ideologically, the very existence of the euro was predicated upon the continental version of neoliberalism: German ordoliberalism. The disciples of this particularly austere church have very precise ideas on how society and economy should work: through strong and independent institutions whose primary goal is to guarantee unhampered competition and market stability. The independent European Central Bank (ECB), devoted to the strict control of inflation—Germany's second-worst historical nightmare—remains the cornerstone of this model. According to this perspective, attempting to reduce public debt through government spending is not only economically unsound, but also morally wrong. As Mario Monti—the technocrat who replaced Silvio Berlusconi as Italy's prime minister in 2011 to handle the economic crisis—put it in several speeches, public debt is the consequence of past sins, and interest rates are the measure of their gravity.[11]

Austerity policies are thus an act of redemption, or, as Mariano Rajoy had it, of "moral sanitization."[12]

This promise of redemption proved a potent disciplinary tool. And yet it probably would not have been powerful enough on its own to keep national governments, faced with an increasingly hostile public opinion, on the austerity track. The threat of punishment would do the rest. In several cases (Ireland, Portugal, Greece) this took the form of conditional loans: austerity was the unnegotiable counterpart of vital financial help from the Troika (ECB, IMF, European Commission). In others, such as Italy and Spain, the threat of sanctions triggered in case of violation of the Maastricht Treaty rules (stipulating that the public deficit and debt cannot respectively exceed 3 percent and 60 percent of GDP) would serve as the stick. No matter that these criteria are purely arbitrary, as any economist would confess to the public. No matter that Germany and France ignored them in the past without triggering EU sanctions. The main objective of the euro's institutional design was always the use of power asymmetries to enforce specific reforms to reshape European economies around the German model: wage moderation, disinflation, competitiveness.

National governments hardly needed convincing on this score: austerity had already won their hearts long ago. Moreover, public opinion was, historically, overwhelmingly favorable to the EU and its symbolic attachment to the common currency. In most countries of the European "periphery"—Spain, Greece, and Portugal above all—European integration had always carried a post-dictatorial, democratic sheen. The "stick," therefore, was rather a gift, as it provided national elites with a justification to carry out the reforms they had been craving for years. After all, it wasn't national leaders doing it to their own citizens—it was EU diktat. In Italy, using the "external constraint" rhetoric to liberalize the country's economy had been fashionable since the 1990s, when the Democratic Party was enthusiastically resorting to this trick.[13] For politicians like Antonis Samaras, Mario Monti, and Mariano Rajoy, austerity was no bitter pill: it was perfectly in line with their own orthodoxy. For others, little persuasion was required. George Papandreou and Matteo Renzi, for instance, exemplars of social democratic converts to the benefits of commodification, simply had to carry out some ideological adjustments. This would turn out to be decisive among the causes of the populist upsurge: alongside the socio-economic consequences of austerity, the ideological convergence of mainstream parties and the center-left betrayal would establish a crucial connection, in protesters' minds, between the crisis of democracy and the crisis of the economy.

TINA'd Out

The real-world impact of the measures, however, was bound to generate discontent. Greece lost a quarter of its GDP in one decade. At its height in July 2013, the unemployment rate reached almost 30 percent. A few months earlier, it had reached a peak in Spain, too: almost 27 percent. Half of Spanish twenty-five-year-olds were jobless. Draconian austerity plans were implemented in the countries hardest hit by the recession and whose public finances were deteriorating fastest. These plans—generally carried out in several tranches, each

reinforcing and deepening the effects of the previous ones—
encompassed many different measures. The most common
were VAT hikes, pension reforms, "flexibilization" of the
job market, "liberalization" of public services, public-sector
wage freezes or cuts, and cuts to unemployment benefits. The
social consequences were plain to see: widened inequalities,
increased poverty, and an overall deterioration in the health
of European citizens. Several years later, moreover, it remains
unclear whether their strictly "economic" effects were positive—the IMF itself would slowly come to doubt the recipes.
In 2020, during the first wave of COVID-19, the population
of the North of Italy would traumatically experience the cruel
effects of liberalization, as the bodies piled up in the corridors
of overcrowded hospitals.

One fact remained beyond doubt. National governments,
back then, knew perfectly well what they were doing and the
damage they were planning to inflict on their own populations.
In December 2011, Elsa Fornero, minister of labor and social
policy in Monti's government of technocrats, burst into tears
when explaining what travails the new pension reform would
impose on citizens. "Common effort" and "collective sacrifice"
had become stock phrases for policy makers. They promised
that the suffering would not be in vain, however: austerity was
to guarantee a swift return to economic growth and to political
credibility for European partners. There was a redemptive spirit
to austerity—pain as a prerequisite to healing.[14]

From Dublin to Athens by way of Madrid and Rome,
governments thereby presented these policies as the only viable
solution. Partisan orientations and ideological differences faded

before the promise of financial soundness. Governments were reacting only as required by these exceptional times. Austerity was purely a matter of economic "common sense," according to which "you cannot spend more than what you earn"—an adage which might well resonate with a family's practical experience of household budgeting, but which becomes flatly wrong when applied to the state. Organic and mechanical metaphors helped depict these policies as a purely technical intervention, aiming at restoring the normal functioning of the body or engine. The conclusion was simple: *there was no alternative.* "Fiscal consolidation," as governments preferred to call it, was both economically sound and morally good.

Few actors were uncomfortable with such fatalism. Some were even eager to depict the economy as an autonomous sphere bearing down on all political decisions. For Mario Monti, for instance, the taming of democratic rule was perfectly in line with the functioning of a modern polity. He developed these ideas in an essay co-authored with French MEP Sylvie Goulard (*On Democracy in Europe: Looking Ahead*), which contains all the primary arguments he repeatedly deployed as Italy's (unelected) head of government. In this view, democracy is inherently plagued by the risk of short-termism and electioneering. It should therefore be mitigated by shielding the deciders from "excessive" electoral pressure and enabling them to take the decisions that meet the interests of the people when these "are at variance with their inclinations," quoting American Founding Father Alexander Hamilton.[15] The role of institutions is thus to protect voters from their own irrationality, and to give policies a long-term scope that might safely contradict voters' immediate needs. Austerity is the most striking example of such a logic, since it consists of sacrificing present well-being in the name of a promised brighter future, and thus requires independent institutions with the capacity to administer the bitter medicine to the patient in his own inter-est—even if it's against his will. In short, too much democracy is harmful and inherently inflationary.

It should come as no surprise that such an antidemocratic view was commonplace among technocrats like Monti and Lucas Papademos, or hard-headed conservatives like Samaras and Rajoy. The center-left, on the other hand, had nothing better to propose than a weaker dose of the same medicine. Beyond their calls for a socially concerted and fairly distributed economic effort, the social democratic parties could articulate neither an alternative interpretation of the crisis nor a different policy response to it. In Greece and Spain, the once-dominant Pasok and Zapatero's socialist party (PSOE) were in charge at the onset of the crisis and implemented the first round of austerity. In Italy, the Democratic Party unanimously backed Monti's technocratic government together with Berlusconi's center-right, thus entering a sort of de facto alliance with the latter. All had a single prescription: austerity.

The defection of social democrats was not unexpected for those who had followed the evolution of party alignments over the past two decades. Social democrats' transformation into social-liberal parties—chiefly liberal, barely social—occurred almost everywhere in Western democracies. In a world now deprived of any serious alternative, social democrats aban-doned their historical role—the progressive socializing of capitalism through democratic means—and rebranded themselves as the "Third Way." Starting in the 1990s under the triumphant leadership of Bill Clinton and Tony Blair, the center-left increasingly endorsed a liberal agenda, hailing the "benefits" of globalization while proposing to mitigate its negative social effects by promoting "equal opportunities" of access to the all-powerful markets. As Przeworski's predictions were coming true and the working class was shrinking, the center-left openly turned its back on those citizens and exclusively championed the middle class's aspirations, including European integration. By the outset of the new millennium, there was no trace left of Kautsky's legacy within the main European center-left parties, from Germany to Spain by way of France and Italy. In the latter, indeed, once the most fertile ground for both revolutionary and reformist hopes, there was really nothing left of the left, as the communists had imploded and the resultant centre-left party was now resolutely centrist, adopting the name and the clothes of the US Democratic Party.

Much more than the recession was at stake. Saving the banks while calling for sacrifices from the population had further destroyed the credibility of political elites. More than recession, bailouts, and austerity per se, it was the convergence of political elites around the latter that opened the fatal breach between a large part of the citizenry and its representatives. In other words, the spark that ignited the fire was *the congestion of the channels of representation in which citizens' demands were classically voiced*. Crucial, in that respect, was the commitment of the center-left to neoliberal policies and discourse: by conveying the idea of a lack of alternative to austerity and giving up on channeling the frustration that it generated, they had irremediably lost their credibility as progressive forces. Yet "democracy depends on choice," meaning that "if a change in government cannot translate into different policies, democracy is incapacitated."[16] This very specific conjuncture thus led to an explosive situation for the ruling elites: the coming together of socio-economic grievances and democratic claims. It was here that the populist moment was born.

In a former bus depot, Podemos organized its first proper event of its campaign for the general election (to be held on November 10) in Madrid on October 13, 2019, in the late morning. The lines in Aniceto Marinas Street outside the event hall were impressive. It soon became clear that not everyone would be able to get in. The crowd stuck outside didn't seem too bothered, though. The atmosphere was relaxed and warm; people of all ages were laughing, joking around, singing. The flags and symbols were purple, relatively discreet. The line turned into a semicircle standing in front of the building and trying to see—in vain—through the tinted windows. It seemed that everyone was going to hang around, enjoy the moment, and wait in the hope of meeting the leader in person. Soon, this hope would be fulfilled. Alerted to the presence of the supporters outside, Pablo Iglesias suddenly walked out of the building, holding a megaphone in his right hand. He wore his usual big smile, ponytail, and casual clothes. He was cheered, almost like a rock star. People started to shout repeatedly: "¡Sí se puede!" (Yes, we can!). He waited patiently until the crowd calmed down.

He then explained that far more people than expected had turned up, so it wouldn't be possible to host everyone inside. He recalled some of his parties' priorities and emphasized the risk of voter demobilization—the November election would be a rerun of the April general election, at the end of which Podemos and the PSOE hadn't been able to agree on the formation of a coalition government. "Vote, and tell your families and friends to vote too." He apologized about the event itself but reassured the audience: it would be broadcast live on Podemos's Facebook page. He then went back inside under the applause of the thrilled crowd. As soon as he disappeared, all the attendees got onto their smartphones.

This scene could have happened in many other places during the 2010s: New York, London, Athens, or Paris. It crystallized almost all the decisive traits of the left's populist turn: the capacity to re-inject enthusiasm and passion into politics, the central role of the leader, the massive use of new technologies, the deployment of a language and symbology that broke from the traditional left. As such, these political parties had taken up the slack of the declining movements of the squares. They built on the legacy of those movements, drawing lessons from their instability, and turning their spirit into ambitious electoral forces aimed at the conquest of executive power.

In the content and style of their claims, they undoubtedly granted a second lease of life to the antiausterity movement. By connecting the issues of structural inequality and crisis management in Western societies, by going beyond the left vs. right cleavage and trying to mobilize around new axes—the people vs. the oligarchy, the many vs. the few, the 99 percent vs. the 1 percent—they endorsed a populist agenda in response to the state of crisis described above. They were not, as such, antisystem—as the Indignados liked to say, it was rather the system that was anti-them. Unlike many strands of the radical left, they were neither against capitalism nor against representative democracy, except for marginal factions within them. Their objective was rather to re-democratize democracy and re-politicize the economy against the concentration of power in the hands of economic and political elites, responsible for gutting the substance of democracy.

There was another side to the story, however. As suggested above, while the movements of the squares were torn between horizontal and vertical approaches, the former almost completely disappeared in the political formations that took up their legacy. Excessive horizontality and inefficient decision-making procedures were now prohibited: the purpose was to conquer power. Times had changed. The populist actors who emerged in the aftermath of the Great Recession were keen to suppress superfluous layers of organization, set up frequent online consultations with their members, adopt modern modes and channels of communication, and rely on a charismatic and telegenic leadership figure. They were ready to embark on the Great Transformation of politics the previous decades had led to.

Disorganized Democracy

"Elections don't change anything." The admission was frank, with a touch of cruelty. Standing in the meeting room of the

Brussels' Lambermont building, the Greek finance minister, Yanis Varoufakis, listened to his German counterpart, Wolfgang Schäuble, explain how it was practically impossible for his party to ever implement the platform they were elected on. Schäuble was unrepentant about his opponent's request to restructure the Greek debt.[17] In one sense, Schäuble was right: elections really did matter less and less. Actual power lay elsewhere, outside of Varoufakis's parliaments, parties, and elected governments—yet where, exactly?

Schäuble was no recent convert to the sentiment either. Thirty years earlier, he had presided over the dismantling of GDR infrastructure after the fall of the Berlin Wall and began the incorporation of Eastern German labor markets into the West, giving West German employers access to an enormous labor pool stretching all the way to the Baltics and the Russian border—the inclusion of "six Liverpools," as an advisor to Margaret Thatcher put it. The fate of the GDR was but a miniature of a global process of capitalist consolidation. From Russia to India to Indonesia, great stretches of the planet suddenly found themselves roped into a global community of the market, subject to changing labor scales and welfare standards.

The year 1989 inaugurated, however, much more than a mere economic restructuring. Across Europe and the United States, the institutions that had ordered and contested industrial capitalism in the post-war period were themselves falling apart, splintering into small sects for hobbyists or disappearing altogether. By 1994, the Italian Communist Party was transforming into a moderate social democratic party. Its former leader Achille Occhetto traveled to Wall Street, declaring its banks "the temple of democracy" and NATO "the center of civilization." On TV the millionaire Silvio Berlusconi, flanked by scantily clothed female presenters, was proclaiming the advent of a "people's capitalism." A capitalist comet had hit the West and killed the dinosaurs: the neoliberal ice age had now properly begun.

Uprooting the Arboretum

The ultimate roots of 1989 were in the 1970s. Already for decades, businesses across the Western world had begun reporting losses to their shareholders. This situation put Western states in a bind. In the post-war period a fragile equilibrium was built between the two warring social factions. Since the nineteenth century, both had engaged in protracted and continuous trench warfare—a war to which fascism provided the bloodiest solution. A more careful integration was agreed on in the aftermath of World War II. Capital had to agree to distribute part of its profits back into state coffers, which would fund working-class consumption. Radical working classes would not meddle with property rights and would leave the ruling class to rule. An intricate list of pacifying civil institutions was set up, from trade unions to mass parties, which sought to make sure that capitalism would grow for, and not against, the working classes. As ever, the presupposition was that the system would deliver perpetual growth—there would always be a bigger and bigger pie to share. By 1968, cracks were appearing in this compact, with industrial workers and young students pining for a jailbreak from the post-war settlement. By 1973, however, the industrial growth motor itself was sputtering: a series of oil shocks hit European economies, which were already suffering from declining profit rates.

The 1973 crash confronted state managers with a tricky dilemma. Unions supposedly kept wages buoyant. This created the danger of an increased money supply and inflation. By 1980, the options were clear: either cut ties with existing civil society organizations and suppress the inflationary threat, or face deep restructuring and ballooning public debt. Ultimately, each country chose its own path out of the crucible of the 1970s, none of them pretty. All of them, however, required breaking the control that organized civil society had over the state, which it used to either redistribute or direct economic resources. A "void" suddenly opened up between society and the state. The latter became a neutral player in the economic game, while in the former, individuals retreated into their own private lives.

Behind the short-term fallout of the credit crisis, then, stood a much longer process: the slow but steady decline of European party democracy since the 1973 slump. The post-war structures that first institutionalized competition between parties after the fascist experience took various forms, all known as a new "organized democracy." In the Netherlands, this compartmentalization referred to the creation of separate spheres for socialist, liberal, and Christian Democratic parties, each with their own newspapers, youth clubs, and even hospitals. In Britain, both Labour and the Conservatives relied on a broad substructure of clubs and trade unions to mobilize their voters. In Eastern Europe, the satellite states of the Soviet Union maintained a one-party system but sponsored civil-society initiatives that laid the foundations for the dissident movement in the 1970s. (In Southern Europe's dictatorships, official party democracy did not experience its honeymoon until later.) Like fortresses built between individuals and their states, these social institutions mediated heavily throughout the twentieth century. As sociologists noted about one social democratic party in the 1930s, the outfit had

> a party organization, a trade union with affiliated theatre club, a child welfare committee called Children's Friends, the Society of Free Thinkers, the Flame (a cremation society), a cycling club, the Workers' Radio Club, the Workers' Athletic Club, the Wrestling Club, the Young Socialist Workers, the Republican Home Guard, the Workers' Library, the Rabbit Breeders' Association, and the Allotment Owners' Association.[18]

On the conservative side, this multiple mediation was bemoaned. The jurist Carl Schmitt already objected in 1927:

> We do not have a total state but a plurality of total parties. Each party realizes in itself the totality, totally absorbing their members, guiding individuals from cradle to grave, from kindergarten to burial and cremation, situating itself totally in the most diverse social groups and passing on to its membership the correct views, the correct ideology, the correct form of state, the correct economic system, and the correct sociability on account of the party. Old liberal-styled

parties, which are not capable of such organization, are in danger of being pulverized by the millstones of the modern total party. The drive towards politicization appears to be inescapable . . . a strong well-organized plural party system interposes itself between the state and its government on the one side, and the mass of citizens on the other, and manipulates the monopoly of politics.[19]

This ordered modernity saw even more explicit expression in the works of the Hungarian intellectual Gáspár Tamás, who described

the creation of a counter-power of working-class trade unions and parties, with their own savings banks, health and pension funds, newspapers, extramural popular academies, workingmen's clubs, libraries, choirs, brass bands, *engagé* intellectuals, songs, novels, philosophical treatises, learned journals, pamphlets, well-entrenched local governments, temperance societies—all with their own mores, manners and style.[20]

Being "total organizations," Tamás's parties were predictably described as modern institutions par excellence. Unlike with the medieval guilds, membership of a party was not obligatory—it was a free association, which members could join to defend their interests. As Antonio Gramsci saw it, the party served as the modern equivalent of the Machiavellian prince, managing complex political situations with tact and insight. This could be done by building up both a base and a framework; parties work from the top down, but also from the bottom up.

The era of high-party politics was never one of irenic stability. In 1958, Charles de Gaulle's coup upset France's republican order and transitioned the country into a presidential regime with softly authoritarian features.[21] In Greece, Spain, and Portugal, populations lived under dictatorships sheltered by a Cold War umbrella. In Britain, mass strikes and worker unrest unseated conservative governments. The notion of a long capitalist peace hid the colonial expeditions and communist counterinsurgency embroiling European empires. Yet these were regimes built, in many ways, on the party state that Schmitt had first lamented in the 1930s, where the working class achieved a much greater say in government than it did before. It was the West's "democratic age," as historian Martin Conway terms it, for better and for worse—the era when the democratic component in "liberal democracy" counted for something.[22]

Over the past thirty years, these pillars of party democracy have gradually eroded and hollowed out. Two trends remain symptomatic of this process. The first is the declining membership of parties across the board, coupled with the increasing age of their members. The German SPD went from 1 million members in 1986 to 660,000 in 2003; the Dutch Socialists went from 90,000 to 57,000. The French Communist Party (PCF) tumbled from 632,000 in 1978 to 210,000 in 1998; its Italian sister party went from 1,753,323 to 621,670 in 1998, only to disappear into the Partito Democratico. The British Labour Party counted 675,906 members in 1978, falling to 200,000 in 2005. (The figure rebounded in 2016 under Corbyn, stabilizing around 400,000, before plummeting again under Keir Starmer.)

While the trend is more marked for the classical left, which has always strongly relied on mass mobilization, it remains no less striking on the right. The British Conservatives lost 1 million members between 1973 and 1994, while the French Gaullists dropped from 760,000 to 80,000. The Tories—the first mass party in European history—receive more donations from dead members than from living ones, excluding Russian oligarchs. Visitors to the British Isles will be struck by the fading colors of the "Conservative Club" signs in English provincial towns. Like the old workingmen's clubs, these hardly function as engines of recruitment anymore and often look more like retirement homes. The median age of Conservative Party members is now estimated at seventy-two.

Not all European states decoupled their states and societies in identical ways. In many countries, several institutions of welfare capitalism were preserved—think of Belgium, the Netherlands, or the Scandinavian countries, whose safety nets and corporatist circuits still prove robust. Across the board, however, even these formations had to contend with the tightening constraints of a flagging capitalism spiraling into stagflation. Many political parties lost their representative role and became mere vehicles for "governance"—ordering society so that capital could comfortably keep on paying its shareholders. As a result, the once mighty Belgian Socialist Party is losing its grip on the industrial working class, which is increasingly seduced by the "authentic left" option put forward by the PTB (Workers' Party of Belgium).

The United States had often acted as an outlier to these European examples. Americans have never had any true mass parties since 1896, the last major examples being the antislavery agitation of the 1850s and the rise of the original Populist movement in the 1880s and '90s, visible in the foundation of the GOP and the People's Party. After Populism was defeated, however—in the South by stuffed ballot boxes and bayonets, in the North by simple electoral dominance—bipartisan elites constructed a system which essentially neutered any third-party challenger. American parties nonetheless had a variety of bases and roots within society. These organizations effectively made them "mass parties" by proxy, tied to a plethora of labor, union, and civil organizations which defended popular interests to apparatchiks. Both on the left and the right, workers, employers, and small businesspeople defended their interests in local clubs, committees, and parties.

This civic landscape was also a key factor in the revolts which culminated in the Civil Rights revolution of the 1960s. Like most of their precedents in the 1930s, all these moments were also driven from a tightly organized and increasingly interracial labor movement: Detroit labor leader Walter Reuther marched with Martin Luther King in the early 1960s, while one of the foremost radical supporters of the 1963 March on Washington was A. Philip Randolph, a black labor leader who had begun by organizing black co-workers under the Jim Crow regime. The relation of these forces to the Democratic Party was persistently complicated and often fractious. Overall, however, they ensured that the party remained a "party of workers" without ever becoming a "workers' party."[23]

From the 1970s, this same landscape began to desiccate, both passively and actively. The Tocquevillian utopia admired by generations of European visitors to the continent was replaced by the reality of "bowling alone." Instead of mass-membership structures, voluntary organizations increasingly turned to a non-profit model to streamline their advocacy in Washington.

The shift to the non-profit also changed the very composition of many of these advocacy groups. Instead of relying on dues-paying members, they increasingly reached out to wealthy donors to fill their coffers. In a federation in which the state was increasingly abandoning its redistributive role, this shift created a natural constituency for new welfare recipients. The logic was clear: associations that practically operated as businesses, but did not want to fulfill their obligations to the state treasury, saw their chance in the non-profit model. The American political scientist Theda Skocpol conceptualized this new civil society as relying on an "advocacy without members": non-profit organizations as the lawyers of a deaf and mute defendant.[24] The similarity with the euro-lobbies, which also swarmed around the remaining member states, was evident.

Process or Protest
Parties came up with two survival tactics in their neoliberal ice age. The first was an increased investment in "public relations"—an industry which mushroomed at the same time as the finance industry, heavily reliant on the same conjectures, speculation, and guesswork. The second was a separation between politics and policy and an increased transfer of power to technocratic bodies.[25] Like any beauty contest, the financial

economy dealt in illusion and make-believe. The right had always been a step ahead in the PR race. Thatcher's notorious 1979 campaign poster— "Labour Isn't Working"—was commissioned from the London advertising firm Saatchi & Saatchi. In the 1980s, the whiz kids found their way to a more left-wing clientele. Labour consultants such as Peter Mandelson also collaborated with the Saatchis, while French socialists began to draw on Parisian fashion designers. As Christopher Hitchens recalled, "When the Tories first hired a public-relations firm called Colman, Prentiss and Varley . . . they got a fair bit of ribbing from cartoonists," while "the Labour Party in those days was sternly opposed to the pseudo-science of PR and polling."[26] By the end of the 1990s, the pupil had outstripped the teacher. PR politics requires funds, of course. But it was generally cheaper, and less organizationally exigent. Rather than rallying thousands of supporters and members in large institutions—members who could also pressure politicians at conferences and meetings—it was smarter to treat the electorate as a black box that could be uncovered a posteriori. Everyone and no one became a potential voter; sociology was traded for public relations. The public's wishes and demands could now be gauged by a professional marketing department.

The recurrent use of the business metaphor hardly came as a surprise here. While political scientists had been discussing electoral competition in terms of "supply and demand" since at least the 1950s, only in the 1980s did politics itself become so openly marketized. Politicians began to relate to their society differently, as well. Instead of representatives defending a sectorial interest, they became entrepreneurs trying to sell a product to a public on which they now projected opinions. "Performance" and appearance became essential attributes for politicians, not simply a means of dressing up party programs.

What about the other antipode of parties—the state? Since the 1990s, there has been a split between two activities that were classically linked in the post-war era: politics and policy. "Policy" stands for the methods by which states organize their societies, such as choosing winners and losers in industrial policy. "Politics" includes the process of what political theorists call "will formation": competition between parties, campaigning, and the forging of coalitions.

In the 1990s, these two spheres began to interact in a radically different way. Policy became the domain of unelected power—bodies such as the Eurogroup, the European Commission, or central banks, including the Bank of England, the Federal Reserve, and the European Central Bank. Politics was left to a media apparatus addicted to novelty, supplemented somewhat hopefully by the internet and its participatory promises. Into this sludge stepped the articulate netizen, laptop at the ready, but without a party card—one of the atomized members of a new, virtual people.

Naturally, this increasing separation of policy and politics also had clear economic drivers. Unsurprisingly, old mass party often compared to the factory floor: both espoused a tight, almost martial organization in which militants and leaders adhered to a well-defined hierarchy and division of tasks. Those parties also defended specific interest groups in society: employees or employers, the middle or upper classes,

Protestants or Catholics. Now to social scientists, instead of workers, there were small and large entrepreneurs, and instead of the proletariat, the so-called precariat. With the slowdown in growth rates since the early 1970s, European economies began to accumulate ever larger public debts. Broadly speaking, the states had two options for dealing with this accumulation crisis: temper the demands of the working class in favor of capital, or temper the demands of capital in favor of the working class. The former's supposed urge to overload the state with demands led to a strong tendency toward inflation, already infamous at the time as the "economic disease of democracy."[27] In the 1970s, most governments kept expectations high by borrowing more public money. This situation provoked a fierce response from capitalists, who were always looking for higher profit margins and worried about the creditworthiness of states. Capital thus began to push for a transition from fiscal to debt states, as Wolfgang Streeck termed them, but also heavily scarred civil society structures along the way.[28] Only through "discipline," whether through self-sufficiency or lower wage and rates demands, could the deadlock be broken. As the political scientist Mancur Olson already concluded at the end of his 1972 *Logic of Collective Action*, social groups could not "be expected to organize or act simply because the gains from group action would exceed the costs . . . Why would the people of this (or any other) country organize politically to prevent inflation when they could serve their common interest in price stability just as well if they all spent less as individuals?"[29] Central banks could raise rates and thereby refigure the economic landscape; flood would turn into drought. But the inhabitants of that landscape had to adjust to the new climate. Reagan's attack on the airliner unions and Volcker's hawkish monetary policy could join hands: it allowed for a slow squeezing of the organizations that supposedly drove the state to spend and increase inflation, and thereby restore conditions for capitalist stability. The capitalist retort was described as follows by the English historian James Heartfield:

> To defeat the working-class challenge of the seventies, the elite tore up the old institutions that bound the masses to the state. Class conflict was institutionalized under the old system, which not only contained working-class opposition but also helped the ruling class to formulate a common outlook. What started as an offensive against working-class solidarity in the eighties undermined the institutions that bound society together. Not just trade unions and socialist parties were undermined, but so too were right-wing political parties and their traditional support bases amongst church and farmers' groups. Middle-class professional groups lost their privileged position.[30]

The process Heartfield charts not only concerns the loss of a group of core voters. The erosion of party democracy is also about the withering away and crushing of a certain civil society: institutions that stand between the citizen and the state and shape the relationship of the citizen *to* that state: trade unions, farmers' associations, churches, neighborhood clubs. Historians repeatedly characterize the Dutch PvdA as a party that had "trunks and roots" all through society, a tree whose branches were visible in every layer of society. In the 1970s, the British House of Commons counted 150 teachers, twenty engineers, and thirty miners among its members, most of whom had come from trade unions or workers' clubs.

The occasionally authoritarian aspects of this social form should not be downplayed. In the 1960s, Flemish and Italian priests could still tell their parishioners who they should vote for on Sunday, while party bosses gave instructions to the editors of their newspapers. The Italian Tangentopoli scandal in the early 1990s unmasked the country's particracy as flamboyantly corrupt. In his memoirs, French philosopher Jean-Claude Michéa remembered that one of the most disconcerting moments of his childhood was the day he discovered that there were people living in the village who were not members of the French Communist Party (PCF). "That seemed to me simply unimaginable," he writes, as if those people "lived outside of society."[31] The borders of the party were the borders of his world. Not coincidentally, in May 1968, French students sometimes compared the relationship of the workers to the PCF with that of Christians to the Church. The Christians yearned for God, the workers for revolution. Instead, "the Christians got the Church, and the working class got the Party."

Above all, the erosion of the party base led to a new performance style among politicians, who adopt a completely different approach to their electorate. They no longer have a party-based constituency that they can call on at every election. For some politicians, this was enthralling, as it enabled parties to reach a wider audience, especially through media campaigns. Tony Blair wanted to get rid of the narrow trade-union vote within

Labour, which seemed to hinder access to an electoral reserve and irritate the middle classes.

Ultimately, the tactic also harbored significant risks: anybody suddenly qualified as a potential voter, while a new, ostensibly "value-free" administration would cover the widening gap between citizen and politics. Some radicals mistook this general disaffection with politics for a renewed mandate for radical action, as if the emptying out of established parties would create a constituency vacated by traditional political forces. Yet this often proved a misreading of the situation. While the departure from large, paternalistic parties amounted to a mass exodus, there was no corresponding voice raised in the world of "bowling alone," or any which induced citizens to reconnect with their representatives.

One pitiful example of this disconnection occurred in the United Kingdom, as the parliamentarian Owen Smith was challenging Jeremy Corbyn for leadership of the Labour Party. When Smith was interviewed in an Italian restaurant in the English North, he pretended not to know the word "latte"— instead calling the drink a "frothy coffee."[32] Smith evidently felt the need to feign authenticity to his constituents. As a Labour MP, he had simply never encountered a real working-class person, who, according to statistics, had in fact been consuming lattes for years.

A narrower party base does not, of course, imply that parties now cede their role as suppliers of policy. Party bureaucrats still work their way up within party structures, but they do so less and less with democratic backing. Since the 1990s, politicians are increasingly drawn from a professional universe, be it academic or business. In place of the union leader or civic tribune, a new figure has come to the fore: the expert. The American sociologist Stephanie Mudge recently called this the "re-professionalization" of party politics, akin to the "diploma democracy" known in the Netherlands.[33] The result is reminiscent of the nineteenth-century politics of dignitaries, but without the haughtiness of the *ancien régime* that shielded the rulers of the day from its rabble. The tree of the party may have been hollowed out, but even a rotten trunk still offers a route to the rewards at the top.

Not everyone felt comfortable with this marketization of politics. On the left, radicals contested the implementation of the new market order and began to take to the streets. Even here, however, an emphasis on "performance" proved all too tempting. The 1998 descent on Seattle and the 2001 antiglobalization protests maintained an emphasis on the visibility of certain signs, even if they counted a sizable union contingent seeking to reduce the labor market pressures induced by globalization and the China shock. These were quickly cornered by more movementist elements, however. Rather than mount assaults in the workplace, however, the left-wing struggle moved to the streets and the square, whose cobblestones were said in 1968 to hide a beach. Underneath those cobblestones, however, there was always something else, as Ralph Miliband pointed out—the sewer.

Here lies the volcanic landscape in which "populism" flourishes. Added to an older social democratic dilemma, the new crisis of political engagement (expressed in declining voter participation and party membership) compounded into an even trickier dilemma for the twenty-first-century left. Not only did it have to weld groups that were more fragmented than ever—rather than Przeworski's binary, the left now faced a scattering of smaller groups with incompatible interests and cultural sensibilities—it also had to contend with an anemic civil society, in which politics itself had been privatized. How to organize for this age of disorganization became the defining quandary of the millennial left.

A new ecosystem also generates opportunities, of course. The abandonment of mass parties and the growing alienation between politicians and citizens can only be temporarily averted with television commercials and marketing stunts. By 2010, it was clear both classical PR and protest politics were falling short of their promises. Austerity was decimating pensions and public sectors across the European South. Public debt, itself channeled by private debt, was rising. In March 2013, a group of Indignados began to meet with professors at the Complutense University in Madrid. One year later they ran for office in the European election and won seats. In France, other activists would reach for the same playbook in late 2016, drawing on the Spanish example. For years, journalists reserved the name "populism" for forces on the right and farther right, often eagerly seconded by right-wing figures; now, figures on the left were plotting their own populist turn. But what did it mean for the left to "go populist"?

3.

EBB AND FLOW

On January 7, 2020, the Spanish Parliament became the stage for a deeply unusual scene: Podemos's leader, Pablo Iglesias, burst into tears after Pedro Sánchez, president of the Socialist Party, was appointed the new prime minister of a coalition government that included his own party. Ten years after the outbreak of the economic crisis in the euro area, almost exactly six years after the creation of Podemos, the political heir of the Indignados finally made it to the national government, so achieving one of the party's stated goals.

Were Iglesias's tears of joy? Not exactly. His political triumph came at high cost: on its way to executive power, Podemos lost 2 million voters, experienced harsh internal tensions leading to the departure of its second-in-command, and gave up on many of its initial aspirations. The alliance of socialists and populists was also the result of long and arduous negotiations initiated nine months earlier, which succeeded only after a risky electoral rerun weakened both leftist parties while reinforcing the far right, thus forcing the former into an unwanted cohabitation. With the ebb of his populist tide, Iglesias found himself as the last man standing, the lucky survivor of a shipwreck, too isolated and exhausted to conquer the new land whose shores he had miraculously reached. As far as the eye could see, mainstream politicians had kept or recovered the upper hand: Syriza had lost power a few months before, and Macron, Biden, Starmer, and Sánchez were at the helm.

For Pedro Sánchez, there was no more cause to fear the populist filibuster. Iglesias had lost most of his crew on the journey, and would not be able to incite a mutiny. The specter of "Pasokification"—named after the abrupt collapse of the Greek center-left party—had already been warded off. Podemos's weakness was the very reason why it finally got into government: the hegemony of the PSOE over the left was no longer in danger. In fact, it now needed an aide-de-camp. There was no international fleet capable of coming to Iglesias's rescue, either: the left-populist tide was receding on both the Mediterranean and the Atlantic. From Athens to DC, the specter that once haunted Western oligarchies now seemed to be nothing but a harmless ghost. For the populist moment of the left, all in all, followed a remarkably similar script in every country: early electoral successes creating high expectations, period of institutionalization marked by public scandals and internal tensions, and relative failure leading to the downscaling of initial ambitions.

We gain a better sense of the left-populist life cycle when we periodize it in two phases. At first, between 2012 and 2017, left populism was on the upswing. In Greece, it succeeded in marginalizing the socialist party and finding its way into the national government in 2015. On the other side of the Mediterranean, it disrupted the two-player game of Spanish politics, won several important municipalities, and seriously threatened to overtake the socialist party at the national level. In France, the explicit adoption of a populist agenda almost won Mélenchon a ticket for the second round of the 2017 presidential election. Meanwhile, in the anglophone world, it handed the keys to Jeremy Corbyn and enabled Bernie Sanders to challenge the establishment of the Democratic Party in the primaries of the 2016 presidential election. These were not autarchic political experiences, however. Each of these movements took inspiration from the others and several transnational alliances saw the light of day—"First we take Manhattan, then we take Berlin," said Tsipras, quoting Leonard Cohen, on an American trip.

From that point on, however, the upward movement stalled. The first setback occurred as early as the summer of 2015. Alexis Tsipras bowed to the demands of his European creditors, thus halting the momentum that brought him to power and condemning his party to go back into opposition after the next general election. The Greek white flag, in turn, created the first tensions between the Spanish corsair and the French, the latter trying to dissociate himself from Tsipras's strategy. It was only a matter of time before they would face disappointing setbacks, too. Podemos experienced its electoral apex in 2015–16—in 2019, it lost half of its seats in Parliament (from seventy-one to thirty-five). Most importantly, it almost imploded in the meantime; it lost its most prominent strategist and former number two, Íñigo Errejón, due to fierce disputes over the party's game plan. La France insoumise (LFI) performed disappointingly in all the elections held after the presidential contest (legislative, local, European). Its leader's reputation was seriously damaged by the controversial episode of the police search of party headquarters. In the UK, Corbyn never succeeded in pushing Labour's results up, in a context overdetermined by the Brexit negotiations, and eventually stepped down from the party leadership. Finally, Bernie failed once more to win the Democratic Party's nomination for the presidency, notwithstanding his four years of preparation and the considerable financial and human resources he relied on during his campaign.

Although all were products of the "void" described by Peter Mair, these attempted incursions were not exactly of the same nature. It is one thing to change the strategy of an existing radical-left formation to move it off the margins; it is quite another to create a political party out of the blue, let alone to storm an established center-left, social-liberal political party. Each of these strategies entails specific challenges. Firstly, that of reconciling ideological positions at odds with each other, managing the inevitable institutionalization of the party-movement, and struggling against powerful allies-cum-adversaries. Among the main left-populist hubs of the decade, all aiming to conquer a broad electoral majority to advance a radical agenda, we can broadly distinguish two sub-groups.

The outsiders, on one hand, attempted this conquest from *outside* the established political formations, either by transforming an existing party or by creating a brand-new one. Mélenchon left the French Socialist Party in 2008 and, from then on, tried his luck three times at the presidential election under different labels (Front de Gauche, France insoumise, Union Populaire).[1] Podemos was created almost out of nothing—barring a pre-existing groupuscule, Izquierda Anticapitalista (Anticapitalist Left)—by a group of academics eager to give a political legacy to the social upsurge of 2011. Syriza, a political coalition born in 2004, relatively marginal during the 2000s, took on a completely different dimension in the context of the euro area crisis and found itself in the national government. On the other hand, for Jeremy Corbyn and Bernie Sanders, creating a third party was hardly conceivable, in a political landscape marked by the longstanding inertia of the main partisan machines fostered by the strongly majoritarian logic of their countries' electoral systems. Accordingly, they both attempted to seize the wheel of the machine, based on a smart combination of grassroots activism and innovative communication strategies.

In this chapter, we will examine the way all these populist contenders, whether from inside or outside the established political parties, moved to disrupt the political status quo and further a radical agenda. We will describe the trajectories they followed, from the onset of their rise to the current situation, at the dawn of a new political cycle opened by the COVID-19 crisis. This is not a mere exercise in sadomasochism, however. Our aim is certainly not to vilify left-populist strategy per se, or to cast a pessimistic light on the present and future of emancipatory politics. Our intention is, instead, to help identify the common pattern underlying the trajectory of left-populist contenders, considering that this pattern might provide decisive information on the conditions for a successful renewal of left-wing politics in an era after mass politics.

Storming Heaven: Populism in the Mediterranean

Betrayal: Syriza Surrenders

> **Pasokification**. *Noun*. Reducing a country's main social democratic party to the smallest party in parliament as a result of the rise of a more radical left party. *Pasokification has already happened to Scottish Labour*. (Definition submitted to the Collins Dictionary, May 14, 2015.)

"The people have sent a strong message: PASOK is here, it has not lost its soul, our target to win the [general] election is reachable." On March 18, 2012, Evangelos Venizelos, the recently elected leader of the Panhellenic Socialist Movement (PASOK), rallied his troops. Two months later, the results were plain: his party suffered a humiliating defeat in that general election, falling from 44 to 13 percent of vote share, losing 119 out of its 160 seats.

It was only the start of his troubles. In a snap election held one month later, the party bled out eight more seats. By January 2015, it had plummeted to under 5 percent of the vote share. Within six years, a proud center-left party in an abidingly stable party system, constructed after a democratic transition, had become virtually irrelevant. Steadily, the word "Pasokification" imposed itself as a de facto signifier of the sudden collapse of a social democratic party (as a punishment for becoming centrist) and the subsequent opening up of a political space to the advantage of an upstart contender on its left. In France and Spain, the term also embodied fresh hope: that a newly populist left could simply overtake social democracy and occupy the place it left vacant.

For the dividends of PASOK's implosion were not distributed equally across the political spectrum. Syriza was by far the main beneficiary of the wipe-out. How come a radical left coalition created in the 2000s—it became a party in 2012—went from getting a modest 4.6 percent of the vote share in 2009 to becoming the first Greek party in 2015? Gathering several small far-left formations around Synapsismos (SYN)—a dissident faction of the Greek communist party (KKE)—Syriza was quite different from the Marxist left from which it had split. It was less firmly tied to the trade unions and closer to the social movements, rooted in the urban middle classes and university students rather than in the organized working class, and displayed a remarkable ideological pluralism. In the context of the financial crisis, these characteristics made Syriza "the right left in the right place": neither stubbornly orthodox nor amorphously centrist.

The crisis set the stage for a new "populist moment." The economic situation was far worse in Greece than in the rest of Europe. While global markets were plunging, the newly elected PASOK government, led by Andreas Papandreou, had inherited a very critical situation with the public finances, leading to the intervention of the Troika. The terms of the deal were very clearly spelled out: the massive loans granted by the creditors to "save the country" would have to be accompanied by a "Memorandum of Understanding" (MoU)—stipulating

(extremely) harsh austerity measures. Meanwhile, debt restructuring would remain as economically ineluctable as it was
politically intolerable.[2] As a result, the Greek predicament
went from bad to worse: GDP fell by 25 percent between
2008 and 2013 and unemployment peaked at 27.5 in 2013,
pushing whole sectors of society into poverty. The public
debt/GDP ratio, on the other hand, continued to increase: by
the end of the 2010s, it still amounted to approximately 185
percent (up from 103 percent in 2007). The weakness of the
economic arguments for austerity had always been evident:
it rather reflected the power asymmetries within the euro
area and the priority given to the protection of French and
German creditors. As Varoufakis saw it, *extend and pretend*
was the only game in town. When Papandreou's resignation
in 2011 required the appointment of a "caretaker" government
supported by all the main political forces, and the signing of
a new memorandum, the entire political class was discredited. As the trust in public institutions and political parties
reached a historic low, the Greek population—drawing on
a time-honored socially combative tradition—took to the
streets. After an initial phase of protest (2009–11), relatively
conventional in its composition and repertoires, the mobilization, following a call to spread Indignados-style protests
to Greece, turned into a massive and heterogeneous popular
movement (Aganaktismenoi) out to denounce the hijacking of Greek democracy.[3] All the conditions were ripe for a
populist upsurge.

Syriza was much better equipped than the communist
party (KKE) to take on the electoral representation of social

discontent. While the KKE, stuck in its own "old-school sectarian vanguardism,"[4] criticized the Aganaktismenoi for their lack of ideological purity and dismissed them as "reformist," Syriza's ideological pluralism, as well as its patient and discreet work with the social movements and infiltration of the antiausterity protests, made it the perfect candidate to embody the protest in the institutional arena. This would not have occurred without a strong dose of political voluntarism, however. If all the contextual elements— Syriza's organizational characteristics, an explosive economic situation, a large and lively popular movement, a sclerotic, clientelist alliance of trade unions and political parties—were the ingredients, Syriza's left-populist strategy was the recipe. Syriza's appeal extended beyond its traditional bastions, reaching virtually every stratum of the population. Instead of calling on the "youth" and the "movements," they began to target a much broader constituency: "the people." All the segments of society frustrated by austerity were now being unified and pitted against the political establishment. Pro- vs. anti-MoU was turning into the main political divide, and Syriza successfully embodied the antimemorandum forces. Syriza's radicality suddenly became fashionable. Pursuing a truly hegemonic strategy, Syriza sensed that a new social majority was taking shape and set out to transform it into a new political majority. From being identified with the protesters, it started to be recognized as their true representative.

The dividends of this strategy were plain to see. From 2009 to 2015, Syriza experienced uninterrupted growth. The "*sorpasso*" or overtaking of PASOK occurred as early as May 2012, when the party reached 16.8 percent of the vote share, jumping to 26.9 percent in the snap election held one month later. The party then became the largest political force, for the first time, in the European election of June 2014. Finally, in January 2015, it reached an impressive result of 36 percent and was able to form an antimemorandum coalition government, led by Alexis Tsipras, with a small right-wing party (ANEL). The sociological composition of its electorate evolved accordingly, as its initial overrepresentation among students and unemployed workers progressively gave way to a much more balanced representation of social groups. The populist turn had demonstrated its viability for an authentic left to take power, and Syriza was its first beneficiary on the Old Continent. Five years after the outbreak of the euro crisis, a radical left party had taken up the gauntlet against the Troika.

Six months later, on July 13, Jean-Luc Mélenchon grilled his aides: "Is there anyone here who truly speaks English?" One week before, a resounding majority of Greeks (61 percent) had rejected via referendum the new memorandum proposed by Tsipras's European "partners." Now Mélenchon had that new memorandum, signed by the Greek government, before his eyes—freshly translated from English. He could not believe what he was reading. Why did Podemos and French communists welcome a total surrender to creditors? He double-checked the text and was forced to face the truth: nothing had been lost in translation. He locked himself in his office for an hour to reflect.[5] When he finally emerged, he publicly gave his support to the Greek government, forced to negotiate "with a gun to its head" and to "accept armistice in the war waged against it."[6] From there on, however, he would draw on the lessons of Syriza's failure and adapt his party strategy on European matters. "Europe, change it or leave it" would become a future slogan, with the threat of Frexit (plan B) dangled as leverage in the renegotiations of the 1992 treaties with European partners (plan A).

This lack of leverage greatly exacerbated Syriza's failure—which was, at the end of the day, inevitable. Many observers were amazed by Tsipras's turnaround after the referendum. Retrospectively, however, the acceptance of the memorandum's terms, given the inflexibility of the Troika and the absence of Grexit as a viable alternative, was the only option available. On the one hand, during the six months of tough negotiation between the sides—notoriously indicted by Yanis Varoufakis, the then finance minister, as a "humiliation" for the democratically elected Greek government[7]—not a single request of the Greeks was accepted by their interlocutors. The Troika and the Eurogroup had ruthlessly blackmailed the Hellenic delegation. They openly raised the specter of bankruptcy and expulsion from the eurozone, an option favored mostly by the Schäuble faction in the European government. On the other hand, Tsipras kept a firm lid on any discussion of exiting the euro, deemed logistically unfeasible—it would have meant years of economic chaos, for which no reasonable politician would want to be blamed—and politically unacceptable, in a country where European integration was deeply intertwined with the process of democratization and economic modernization.[8]

This outcome leaves the question as to why the Greek government decided to call a referendum on the new memorandum in the first place. Did it really think that this would have strengthened its position? If "elections could not be allowed to change economic policy," according to the former German finance minister Wolfgang Schaüble, why would a referendum change anything? Perhaps the consultation was directed more toward the inside than the outside. Tsipras had always been a pragmatist. He had certainly understood long ago that his only option was surrender. In this scenario, the referendum was part of a longer blame game, to persuade the leftist faction within Syriza and the Greek population that he was implementing austerity against his will, and that Syriza's government would still be the best guarantee of a socially acceptable "fiscal consolidation." The snap election held two months later proved him right, as he managed both to get rid of the leftist wing of his party and to confirm his position as leader of the majority (Syriza lost only four out of its 149 seats in Parliament). He had fulfilled a grim but realistic dream: Syriza had been turned from a minoritarian gathering of leftist groups into a party of government.

The magnitude of Tsipras's about-face made any radical posture instantly obsolete, however. It was difficult for Syriza to maintain the antiestablishment tone that had brought it to office in the first place. In its first term in government, from January to September 2015, it managed to sell the idea that it was *in office* but not *in power*.[9] Plus, its confrontation with the Troika revived a sense of dignity among large sectors of the population hit by the crisis. In its second mandate,

Syriza's outward face changed dramatically. After attempting a "parallel program" of protective measures toward the most vulnerable sectors of Greek society—unsuccessfully, since the European partners were hostile even to these—it picked fights that were easier to win, such as the "moral war against corruption" and the postmaterialist reforms (immigrant rights, same-sex marriage and adoption, etc.). Tsipras and his team adopted a pragmatic, managerial style, implementing austerity "with social sensitivity" while still referring to a corrupted establishment they were determined to fight. At the end of a four-year mandate, Syriza returned to opposition and saw the right-wing New Democracy Party (ND) form a new government. Considering what it had gone through, its showing in the July 2019 election was surprisingly strong. With 31 percent of the vote share, Syriza remained by far the second largest party; this confirmed its ability to establish itself as an enduring political force within the Greek political system and the main alternative to the right. Even in terms of voting base, Syriza's electorate now looked "less like the popular base of a left-wing party than the 'de-ideologized' clientelist support of a party of government."[10] Syriza was the new PASOK.

At the close of the crisis cycle, the Greek laboratory of left populism appears, to some extent, as the theater of a failed experiment—in Yanis Varoufakis's words, "a bigger blow to the left than Thatcher."[11] Beside the extremely adverse external circumstances specific to the Greek crisis context, Syriza has also undeniably suffered from severe internal limitations. To its credit, and *contra* a certain radical left in love with defeat, Syriza deployed an authentically hegemonic strategy designed to conquer executive power. In doing so, however, it subordinated its praxis to exclusively electoral aims. That strategy comes with evident risks. First, its excessive voluntarism made it relatively blind to the European structure of power relations and the real room for maneuver at its disposal. Second, it endured a rapid process of internal centralization that made it ever more dependent on the figure of its leader, Alexis Tsipras, to the detriment of its originally pluralist and horizontal organizational features. Third, while a healthy dose of pragmatism was the best antidote to sectarian tendencies, its inverse was a tendency for opportunism, which transformed "Let's dare to govern" into "Let's govern at any cost." Overall, and without blaming all of Syriza's failures on the populist strategy, many of Syriza's stumbling blocks prefigured the deadlocks of Europe's left-populist wave as a whole—thus suggesting that their populist nature might also have something to do with their setbacks.[12]

The Failed Sorpasso: Podemos

On May 4, 2021, a few days before the tenth anniversary of the Spanish square movement (15-M), Pablo Iglesias appeared in front of journalists with a grim expression on his face. Behind him stood about fifteen cadres of his party, looking disheartened. The results of the regional election in Madrid had just come out. Podemos had secured a disappointing 7.21 percent of the vote and ten seats out of 136, after a campaign marked by threats of violence from the far right, targeting Iglesias himself. Slightly better than two years prior, the results still lagged far behind their historic showing in 2015, when the party was in a strong third position with 18.64 percent of the vote and twenty-seven seats in the regional assembly. But that was another era entirely, back when bright times lay ahead for *los morados* (the purple party), led by their charismatic leader and his loyal first lieutenant, Íñigo Errejón. Now Iglesias had to taste the bitterness of electoral marginality: his move to step down as the country's deputy prime minister—to rescue Podemos from certain defeat in Madrid—had failed miserably, and the right was now the indisputable leading force in the Spanish capital. As a result of his personal failure, Iglesias decided to leave institutional politics and to step aside in favor of Yolanda Díaz, the new rising star of the Spanish radical left. His comment: "When your role within your organization and your task to improve democracy in this country becomes greatly limited and mobilizes the worst elements of those who hate it, certain decisions must be taken without hesitation."

Seven years before, however, a similar electoral outcome had failed to generate this degree of frustration. It had instead opened a whole new political horizon. On May 25, 2014, Podemos, a brand-new political formation officially created two months earlier, surprised everyone by getting 7.98 percent of the vote share and five seats on its first electoral participation. Picking European elections as the first battleground was a smart move: in political scientists' jargon, these are second-order elections, which tend to be less favorable to mainstream parties. Podemos's founders, among them several professors and students from the Complutense University in Madrid, were perfectly aware of that. They also sensed that behind its apparent stability, the Spanish party system was crumbling. The harshness of the economic crisis and the bipartisan commitment to austerity—indeed, Zapatero's socialist government was the first to implement austerity measures and to introduce the "golden rule" of financial stability within the Spanish constitution (article 135)—had considerably weakened the post-Franco permissive consensus. The astounding social energy of the Indignados, however, seemed to be on the wane, brought to the edge of exhaustion by several years of conservative governance. At the onset of a new electoral cycle (the European elections in 2014, the general and regional elections in 2015), it seemed that no political force could challenge the political establishment, which felt confident enough to urge the protesters to "pursue their objectives through votes, rather than with placards alone."[13] In January 2014, a manifesto calling to "convert indignation into political change" was presented in Lavapiés, a popular neighborhood in Madrid; it would serve as the blueprint for the creation of Podemos. The elites had been taken at their word.

The emergence of Podemos stands as a true "instruction manual" for the creation of a new, competitive political force in times of acute crisis.[14] At its inception, it united partisans of the anticapitalist left (Izquierda Anticapitalista), social activists, and politicized academics, united by their desire to use the political window of opportunity opened up by the 15-M movement and their disappointment with the inertia of the orthodox radical left party, Izquierda Unida (IU). The sources of inspiration for the party's intelligentsia were quite unusual for the European left. Politically, they admired the successes of the Latin American "pink tide" in the 2000s (Hugo Chávez in Venezuela, Evo Morales in Bolivia, Rafael Correa in Ecuador, etc.). Theoretically, they had a predilection for Ernesto Laclau's theory of populism, Antonio Gramsci's thoughts on hegemony, and Carl Schmitt's conceptualization of the political. In this vein, Podemos's first phase consisted of an explicit application of a populist strategy in response to what they called the "Latin Americanization" of Spain—characterized by the pauperization of the middle class, the rise of inequality, the collusion between political and financial elites, the erosion of traditional parties, and the consequent "fluidification" of political labels. The *podemitas* were extremely ambitious: their stated goal was to translate the new "common sense" inherited from the Indignados into a political force capable of winning elections, occupying state institutions, and providing a radical alternative to neoliberalism. *Ganar*—winning—was the keyword of this "populism without apology."[15]

To win, they had to break with both "infantile" (sectarianism) and "senile" (bureaucratism) disorders, which prevented the old left— IU and trade unions were largely seen by the protesters as part of the establishment—from taking up the representation of the widespread social discontent.[16] This implied several drastic operations. First, Podemos distanced itself from the usual language and symbolism of the left. No red flags, hammer and sickle, or "Internationale" in its meetings. The main political frontier was not drawn between capitalists and workers, but rather between "the caste" and "the people."

The message had to be as universal as possible, to reflect the heterogeneity of the social movement and reach voters outside the natural hunting grounds of the left. It was intended to speak the language of the protesters themselves—whose grievances were mainly expressed in terms of unsatisfactory democratic representation ("real democracy now," "they do not represent us," "we are the 99 percent," etc.)—while avoiding potentially divisive issues (antimonarchist stances had to be toned down, for instance). Second, Podemos adopted a hybrid model of organization capable of being inclusive and efficient at the same time—at least on paper. On the one hand, participation on the ground was ensured through local "circles" (*círculos*) and intensive use of the internet. This "movementist" approach aimed at putting into practice the horizontal impetus of 15-M—even though the very creation of a political party with electoral goals was rejected by many Indignados. On the other hand, Podemos embraced an extremely vertical and centralized form of organization, led by a widely recognized figure. The face of Pablo Iglesias, whose notoriety thanks to TV would help the movement gain visibility, was on the ballot papers for the European elections. The idea came from Íñigo Errejón, campaign manager at the time. Both would champion the winning motion during the first national Congress of the party in the fall of 2014 (Vistalegre I), which confirmed and reinforced the vertical orientation of the *morada* formation, justified by the need, in these historic times, to give absolute priority to the electoral struggle (known as *el asalto al cielo*, the storming of heaven). Four hundred days before its first-ever participation in a general election, Podemos boasted a charismatic general secretary at the head of a very disciplined organization.

The stakes were high. By the end of 2014, at the dawn of an intense electoral year, Podemos was neck and neck with the two mainstream parties, PP and PSOE. For a couple of weeks it was even polling at 27 percent, which would have made it the strongest party in Spain. In May 2015, in council elections, Manuela Carmena and Ada Colau, at the head of respective citizens' platforms supported by Podemos (Ahora Madrid and Barcelona en Comú) conquered the two major cities, Madrid and Barcelona. The race for the general election, to be held on December 20, was on. It would be marked by a rapid succession of tough challenges for Podemos: the fierce hostility of the media and its accusations of covert links with the Venezuelan regime, the revived salience of the Catalan issue, the first internal discrepancies over the Madrid-centered management of the party's territorial diversity. Most importantly, the second half of 2015—and singularly the regional election in Cataluña on September 27—saw the arrival of a new contender, Ciudadanos (Citizens). Led by Albert Rivera and speaking the language of "newness" against same-old politics, this sort of business-friendly version of Podemos was poised to attract the voters who were calling for political change but were frightened by Podemos's radicalism. By the time of the Catalan election, Podemos had lost ground to the two traditional parties and had even fallen behind the new outsider in the polls. It would take an extraordinary electoral campaign, dubbed *remontada* ("catching up"), just to come in third place: with more than 5 million votes (20.66 percent

of the vote share, sixty-nine deputies and sixteen senators),
Podemos affirmed itself as the third political force in Spain,
just behind the Socialist Party. The much-awaited *sorpasso*
was in sight.

Who could have imagined, at this point, that the golden
age of the "Podemos hypotheses" was already over? After the
gentle night of "20-D," thorny issues started to arise. How
should the party handle its own exponential growth (risk of
bureaucratization)? What would be the main task of its huge
contingent in the Assembly (risk of institutionalization)? And,
most importantly, what kind of alliances should the party
establish, and what attitude should it adopt vis-à-vis the rest
of the left (risk of normalization)? These issues would soon
tear the party apart. A toxic mix of personal suspicion and
political divergence opened a fratricidal struggle between the
"pablistas" and the "errejonistas"—the respective followers of
Iglesias and Errejón. Beside the clashing personal ambitions
of the two leaders—each of them intimately convinced of
being the true architect of Podemos's successes, the former
as its figurehead and the latter as its mastermind—they were
increasingly divided on key strategic issues. While both sensed
that the populist moment was slowly ending, the window
closing, they diverged on the best strategy going forward. For
Iglesias, Podemos needed to dispute the PSOE's hegemony
on the left through a combative, intransigent attitude, while
keeping one foot in the streets and the other in the institutions.
In Errejón's view, Podemos needed to aim for the political
center, by showing its institutional, consensual, and responsible face—thus being more open to governing in alliance

with the socialists—in order to maintain its wide appeal and avoid being sidelined on the left of the mainstream. The prevalence of Iglesias's view—already discernible in the internal reorganization of the party in March 2016—had two major consequences: a hard line in the negotiations with the PSOE, ultimately leading to the failure of a center-left government investiture, and the creation of a coalition with IU (Unidas Podemos, Together We Can) for the subsequent rerun of the general elections in June 2016. Combining forces, it was thought, would enable them to overtake the socialists and thus put Podemos in a stronger negotiating position to form a progressive government.

Yet politics is not arithmetic. The growth did not materialize: the coalition lost 1 million voters. The socialists, on the other hand, did not "Pasokify." They were still one point ahead. The big winner of the rerun was the conservative right, able to form a second Rajoy-led government with the active support of Ciudadanos and, after a lot of hemming and hawing, the decisive abstention of PSOE. No matter how hard Podemos strove to blame the socialists for the failure to form a progressive government, many voters would never forgive them for paving the way for the Popular Party's return to power. Podemos was never to regain its previous electoral strength. Rather, it endured a slow but steady decline in the polls, while the PSOE, partly thanks to the left turn operated under the leadership of Pedro Sánchez, steadily improved its polling before taking power once again in 2018.

Several elements contributed significantly to this rescaling of Podemos's aspirations. First, the internal disputes got nastier.

The spectacle of the rivalry between Iglesias and Errejón became increasingly damaging to the party's image. The second national Congress of the party (Vistalegre II), held in February 2017, saw their open confrontation and the ruthless victory of the former, prompting the disgrace of the latter, replaced by Irene Montero as spokesperson of the parliamentary group. Less than two years later, the split was complete. Errejón competed in the local elections in Madrid under a separate label—the newly created Más Madrid (More Madrid), supporting Mayor Manuela Carmena, and later to become a national political party (Más País, More Country)—and resigned from his post as a Podemos MP.

Second, from late 2015 onward—and significantly before the Catalan referendum in October 2017—the Catalan issue became a terrible thorn in Podemos's side. The intermediate position taken by its leaders, although motivated by a sincere conception of Spain as a diverse and "plurinational" state, put them in the delicate position of losing despite being correct. At the highest moment of tension, they came to be regarded with suspicion by both the pro-independence and pro-unity camps, and lost a lot of backing from both sides. Third, the eruption of Vox onto the political landscape—first on its Andalusian shore, then country-wide —as a nationalist, reactionary response to mounting regionalist aspirations, reshuffled the cards by totally replacing the old left–right axis at the heart of the political game. In this new configuration, deprived of its novelty by Ciudadanos, edged out by the regenerated socialists, and now faced with the specter of neo-Francoism, Podemos was assigned to the left end of the ideological spectrum. Finally, the scandal that erupted in 2018 over the luxury home that Pablo Iglesias and his partner, Irene Montero, bought outside Madrid interrupted the honeymoon between leader and base. Podemos's discourse on the "casta" was backfiring; even though an internal consultation reconfirmed Iglesias as the legitimate leader of the party, the rot had set in and would be avidly exploited by the media and political rivals.

Podemos would never return to its 2016 level. The increasingly indissoluble coalition with IU declined steadily in the polls, stabilizing at between 10 and 15 percent of the vote. In 2018, an umpteenth corruption scandal got the better of the conservative government. But it was the socialists who were the main beneficiaries of Rajoy's fall, as he was replaced by a minority government led by Pedro Sánchez and ruling with the ad-hoc support of Podemos on specific issues, including a budget agreement on a substantial increase of the minimum wage. By the time this episode was over and the Spaniards were back at the polls, on April 28, 2019, the power balance between the socialists and the *podemitas* overwhelmingly favored the former (28 percent vs. 14, 123 seats vs. forty-two). Both parties, having tried to blame each other for the failed coalition talks after the election, fell slightly in the rerun held in November 2019 (120 seats vs. thirty-five). Faced with the return of the PP and the threatening rise of the far right (Vox had doubled its number of seats in the interim and was now well ahead of Podemos), the left parties reached an agreement in two days. Within a month, Pedro Sánchez was enthroned as the president of the first coalition government since the democratic transition.

Podemos was allotted five portfolios out of twenty-three, with Iglesias serving as second deputy prime minister.

Six years after its appearance on the Spanish political scene, Podemos had finally entered national government—but from the weakest possible position. Most important, the party was barely recognizable. From a populist party hostile to the whole party system and bent on winning an overall majority, it progressively "normalized" and transformed into a restored version of the Spanish radical left, albeit electorally stronger than its European counterparts. Under the new circumstances of Spanish politics—competition between two fragmented poles, left and right—the only available strategy for this Izquierda Unida 2.0 was that of constant haggling with the socialists from a minority position. At the policy level, Podemos can boast of several achievements—a 22 percent increase in the minimum wage, public rent control, and pensions indexation. At the organizational level, it consolidated its structures and territorial anchoring, while becoming more homogenous internally—especially after the exit of the Anticapitalistas branch, in February 2020, seeing off the last competing faction to Iglesias's majoritarian line within the party. Still, nowadays the party looks nothing like its origins—the scrappy mass organization that once threatened to abolish the neoliberal agenda within Spain's borders.

Shrinkage and Expansion: La France insoumise

The only task we should give ourselves is that carried out by Sisyphus: the rock falls back into the ravine, we haul it up again!

On the April 10, 2022, after the provisional publication of the first-round presidential election results, Jean-Luc Mélenchon delivered yet another resounding speech to a crowd. Never had defeat sounded so much like victory. The overall balance sheet was anything but reassuring: after five years of neoliberal therapy, French citizens were, once again, presented with a lesser-evil choice. For the second time in a row, the second round of the presidential election would see a face-off between the extreme center and the far right. Equally for the second time in a row, the country's pro-market forces had an all too handy disciplinary tool to wield against left-wing voters: it's either us or neo-fascist oblivion. Despite the alarms sounded by the establishment—to which the specter of the far right is always useful—the conclusion was obvious: Macron would be comfortably re-elected and would pursue the dismantling of France's welfare state. No reason to bluster, then.

It would have been unwise to feign depression. Despite the bitterness of the outcome—with 22 percent and 7.7 million votes, he was only 420,000 votes away from a duel with Macron—Mélenchon was careful not to repeat the mistake he had made five years earlier. At that time, having come up short at the polls, he had refused to issue voting recommendations to followers, and did not reach out to the rest of the left with the next parliamentary elections in mind. To many sympathizers, this was the original sin that let part of his 2017 political capital go to waste against Macron. This time, he did exactly the opposite: galvanizing his troops, warning three times, and loudly, "not to cast a single vote for Le Pen!" and initiating immediate negotiations with socialists, ecologists, and communists to put together a coalition for the parliamentary elections, the *législatives*. This time, the abyss did not stare back.

What did France see when it began looking at Mélenchon's latest party, however? Rather than a conglomerate, La France insoumise (France Unbowed) has, from the outset, displayed the physical properties of gas: expansive, flexible, but also volatile. When launched on February 10, 2016, it was an unidentified political object. It was created by Mélenchon and a few allies to bypass the rigidities of the Parti de Gauche (Left Party), a structure that Mélenchon had also set up several years before, just after he left the Socialist Party to protest its pro-market, pro-EU orientation. No clear status, no local branches, no national congress, no executive board: LFI had none of the hallmarks of a political party in any traditional sense of the term. Instead, Mélenchon's "movement" was organized around a dozen or more general principles, displayed a sophisticated manifesto unanimously praised for its precision and credibility (*l'avenir en commun*—"the future in common") and enhanced mobilization tactics working with so-called "action groups" across French territory.

This extremely fluid organizational model—in the words of its founding father, it was neither horizontal nor vertical but rather "gaseous"—was designed with two primary goals in mind: it was to provide a platform for supporting Mélenchon's candidacy and breaking down the barriers that hamper popular participation in classic forms of party organization. Jean-Luc's unquestioned leadership was the counterpart to his unwieldy spirit. In line with a famous anarchist critique of "participative democracy tools," LFI's decision-making process could be summarized as follows: "I participate, you participate, they decide." Lacking explicit statutes and procedures, the reality of LFI's model was painfully plain in practice: all decisional power lay with Mélenchon and his inner circle. "*Le parti, c'est moi*"—I'm the party. There were many reasons for setting it up this way. Officially, it was sold under the guise of efficiency and inclusivity: once everyone had agreed to the manifesto, internal battles would do little but drain precious resources and discourage working people from joining the outfit. Unofficially, it responded to a series of personal political traumas undergone by Mélenchon himself, who had spent most of his career as a dissident within the Socialist Party and witnessed its sectarian struggles throughout the Mitterrand years, pitting competing factions and interests against one another.

The results of the 2017 presidential election appeared to vindicate this strategy. After a remarkably efficient and savvy campaign, Mélenchon snatched up 19.58 percent of the vote, just a hair's breadth short of what was needed to reach the second round. Never since 1969 had a radical left candidate gotten so close to the final stage of the presidential contest. The candidate's formidable qualities as a tribune, combined with the advantages of LFI's organizational model—perfectly suited to an extremely personalized election—brought about this unexpected outcome, far above what was forecast and dwarfing the 11.10 percent obtained in 2012. Mélenchon's individual performances during the campaign were etched into the public's memory: technological fads (holograms), trouncing of adversaries in televised debates, vibrant speeches to the masses. As a sixty-six-year-old communist activist expressed in an interview: "I went to several meetings, several speeches, I had tears in my eyes . . . This guy, he's given the people back its dignity."[17]

Mélenchon's gamble also paid off organizationally. Much like the gaseous substance it was often compared to, Mélenchon's movement radically dilated under rising temperatures. Even though it is difficult to know the exact number of adherents, credible sources estimate that LFI grew exponentially over the course of the presidential campaign.[18]

As dedicated Machiavellians, the "Mélenchonistes" also knew that politics is equally divided between *virtù* and *fortuna*. The terrain on which Mélenchon and his squad deployed their talents was indeed hospitable. As in Greece and Spain, a populist window had clearly opened. Even without an economic crisis of Mediterranean proportions, France was going through its own crisis of representation—a malaise accompanied by a concomitant loss of credibility across the "broad center," the center-left and the center-right. For one thing, François Hollande's mandate had proved nothing but catastrophic for the left. After some rhetorical swagger against international finance and European fiscal padlocks, he rapidly surrendered to austerity and enacted pro-business policies (with the El Khomri law), while a series of violent jihadist attacks were used to justify the introduction of harsh naturalization policies. In his final weeks in office, his approval ratings were so low that he decided not to run for re-election—the first time in the history of the Fifth Republic that an incumbent had not attempted a second term. To make matters worse, François Fillon, the odds-on favorite to succeed him—in the bipolar French political system, the candidate of the center-right party (Les Républicains) was automatically seen as the natural opponent and potential successor—was in the doldrums. Halfway through his electoral campaign, "Penelopegate" erupted: Fillon was accused of having generously paid his own wife with public money for a no-show job as a parliamentary assistant. Reneging on his promise, he persisted with his candidacy regardless of the formal investigation. The cut was too deep: eventually, despite initially excellent odds, he would not make it to the second round of the election.

As these players exited the stage, new opportunities cropped up. Emmanuel Macron, a former minister under Hollande, from whom he had distanced himself, had created his own pop-up movement. As a young minister, he stood for election outside of the traditional parties on the promise of political renewal and economic modernization. He managed to rally the centripetal forces of the French party system around a "radical-center" project, openly social-liberal in its content and supposedly new, technocratic, and youngish in its form. Macron's breach further tore open the Fifth Republic's clogged channels and created even more space for contenders. While the far right had a recognizable label and a reliable candidate—Marine Le Pen, 17.90 percent of the vote, had reached the best score of the National Front's history in 2012—Hollande's disastrous tenure produced a heap of ruins. The left had lost any natural leader.

More dangerously, the very signifier of "left" had become virtually unspeakable in the wake of Hollande's imbroglio. In this context, Mélenchon opted for a resolutely populist approach and distanced himself from the language and the symbols of the left. The l-word disappeared from the candidate's electoral platform. The national anthem ("La Marseillaise") replaced the "Internationale" at meetings. The campaign cast its net as wide as possible, targeting slices of the electorate disaffected by the traditional parties. Most of them had turned abstentionist or became romantically involved with the far right (*les fâchés pas fachos*, a French play on words meaning that not all angry voters are necessarily fascists). "Get them out" was the main message: the broad scope of the election was to reclaim popular sovereignty from oligarchic capture. Whereas 2012 was Mélenchon's Syriza/Die Linke moment—the Left Front (a gathering of the Left Party, the French Communist Party, and several smaller left forces), in the name of which he competed in 2012, was inspired by the Greek and German left's coalitional models—this time, Podemos was the main source of inspiration. The French left was taking its populist turn.

The party's April 2017 results proved heartening, but not encouraging enough. A string of subpar performances followed. As Mélenchon's entourage had to admit, they had not thought past the presidential election. Hence, the clumsy press conference after the first round and the dull campaign for the parliamentary elections. These (relatively decent) results were met with a mixed reception. On the one hand, as is customary in the Fifth Republic, the newly elected president obtained a comfortable majority in Parliament. The left in turn was penalized by working-class abstention rates. On the other hand, LFI's score proved sufficient to form a parliamentary group, granting much-needed resources and a more recognizable public image to the organization. Five years of hard legislative work could yield experience and credibility.

At first, it sounded like excellent news. Even opponents heaped praise on the LFI delegation's frenetic activity. In its second, declining phase, however, the once self-described "gaseous" organization finally congealed and condensed. The flow of internal resources was almost completely culled by the seventeen MPs, who tacitly became the movement's executive board—thus generating much tension with the non-elected cadres who felt sidelined and were worried about the dwindling activity of the movement outside of the institutions. The draining of resources away from the ground by the movement's most ossified part was fostered by organizational shrinkage: once the presidential spike was over, lacking more solid party structures many militants trickled out and returned to their daily working lives. As quickly as it had coagulated, Mélenchon's gaseous substance evaporated.

Soon, the movement would face a different set of contenders—outside, in the open air, rather than in the party itself. In late 2018, French men and women began to gather on squares and roundabouts to protest a new round of economically punitive tax hikes. The protesters' style quickly moved beyond a pure tax riot and began to target the haughty, antidemocratic arrogance of the Macron regime. Here was a wide, cross-class mobilization that openly used the language of popular sovereignty. The populist insurrection LFI had repeatedly called for was finally taking shape. As a leaderless Fronde, the Yellow Vest movement also proved remarkably difficult to capture or to capitalize on. LFI never succeeded in translating the movement in the political arena; in fact, both sides looked upon each other with circumspection. While LFI was slow to express solidarity with the movement—which, especially in its initial phase, displayed openly Poujadist traits—it was, in return, regarded suspiciously by the insurgents, who were explicitly hostile to any form of representation. That hostility itself was unsurprising. In the void opened by a failing party democracy, LFI suddenly appeared as just another part of the problem, simply another elite in waiting. Off the record, many cadres castigated LFI for losing touch—except for a few individual figures such as François Ruffin—by its rapid assimilation into France's governing class.

Across 2018 and 2019, debates surged within the movement, leading to the voluntary departure or expulsion of several important cadre members, including Djordje Kuzmanovic, François Cocq, and Charlotte Girard. Their complaints were similar. Each denounced a profound lack of party democracy, hindering serious discussion of LFI's strategy—which, according to these cadres, was moving away from its populist and sovereigntist approach toward a more traditional "leftist" agenda. In the absence of any space for collective deliberation, the discussions regarding the movement's strategy were increasingly restricted to informal meetings between Mélenchon and his inner circle at the Assembly.

LFI's autocratic setup was made even more problematic as, stuck between presidential contests, Mélenchon proved even less capable of herding everyone into his "community of charisma."[19] His temper, a formidable instrument on campaign, turned into a weakness when it came to LFI's daily management. Mélenchon's histrionic reaction to a police search in LFI's headquarters in October 2018, like his response to internal criticism in the June 2019 general assembly, strengthened the sense of malaise among militants. When the movement was actively campaigning for the 2019 European elections, it was able to keep the lid on this discontent. After the disappointing electoral results—LFI secured only a meager 6.31 percent of the vote—backstage disputes flared out into the open. At the close of 2019, shortly before the pandemic struck, the LFI army was in a sorry state of disarray.

Driven into a corner, Mélenchon's spleen began to show. By the end of 2021, he had rebooted his campaign for the presidential election. To the skeptics who pointed out his weakness (he polled only slightly below 10 percent at that time), he retorted that he was much stronger than when he started his campaign in 2017. He was, admittedly, still best placed among potential left candidates. Kicking off his campaign far earlier than his adversaries, he developed a narrative in which he depicted himself as the "sagacious tortoise," who proceeded slowly but surely. To make up for the relative loss of popularity of his movement, he sold his new campaign as part of a much broader platform, "Nous sommes pour" ("We stand for"): first, to support his personal candidacy and promote a rewritten draft of the manifesto, then "L'Union populaire," conceived as a structure enhancing the rallying and participation of civil society figures through an assembly format.

Among these new, post-mass parties, the very function of political organization had changed: they were no longer about entrenching voting blocs over the long run, but rather about providing the best disposable tool adapted to each specific electoral contest. From there on, Mélenchon rose steadily in the polls. His potential left competitors—socialists, ecologists, communists, and Trotskyists alike—began to waver. As the gap widened, it became increasingly clear that he was the only left candidate with a real chance of reaching the second round. This yielded some extraordinary alliances, and kicked off talks with the rest of the leftist forces in France. In the couple of weeks following the presidential election, the French left reached a milestone which for the past twenty years had seemed impossible: a broad electoral alliance between "unbowed," socialists, ecologists, and communists under a single umbrella, the Nouvelle Union Populaire Écologique et Sociale (New Ecologist and Social Popular Union, or NUPES). Much like the agreement between the PSOE and Podemos in Spain, it illustrated the reversal of an old saying: there is more unity in strength than strength in unity. Once again, however, the results proved heartening but not heartening enough: although the coalition succeeded in sabotaging Macron's majority in the Assembly, it failed to obtain an alternate majority to force cohabitation. Meanwhile, the far right increased its presence in the Assembly.

Bring Out Your Dead: Populism in the Atlantic

Crashing the Party: Corbynism
"I own this disaster," the shadow chancellor muttered as he faced the cameras on the evening of December 15, 2019. John

McDonnell's mood was catatonic. On the screens, news was coming in of a blue avalanche in red areas, washing away all the hard-won gains of the last five years of political base-building. Labour had placed a bet—and lost. A changing of the guard was imminent, and the former shadow Brexit secretary, Keir Starmer, was sharpening the knives for a leadership election.

For a while there, McDonnell had seemed to defy gravity. Few movements have enjoyed such unlikely success as the Corbynite wing of the British Labour Party of the last five years. It had started off as more of a tactical gambit than a principled proposal, with several Labour MPs putting Jeremy Corbyn on the ballot for leader in 2015. The idea was merely to steer the overall tenor of the discussion leftward. Yet the increasing hollowing out of the party had also conjured up spirits that proved hard to control by moderate forces. The 2008 credit crash and the ensuing half a decade of austerity measures from the Conservatives (in power since 2010) had spawned a generation faced with skyrocketing rents, stagnating wages, and decrepit public services in what was once one of Europe's most generous and robust welfare states. This generation could neither forgive nor forget. Young people began to flock to Labour's membership rolls in their thousands.

Put forward for merely tactical reasons by party leaders in 2015, the democratization of the leadership contest fueled this influx of new party members. In 2017, Corbyn vied for power with Theresa May and achieved 40 percent of the vote, the largest voting increase for Labour in the post-war period. Strategic ambiguity on the Brexit question had kept both Northern Brexiteers and more Remain-inclined voters inside the tent.

Three years later, Corbyn was out of power and a new group of moderates reclaimed the helm. In its "long jump over the institutions," Labour's focus was firmly electoral and sought to recover a unicameral parliament. Without constitutional strictures, Corbyn's program would prove even easier to implement than its left-populist counterparts. Yet Corbynism, too, was part of a broader wave of revolt.

Like other left-populist phenomena, Corbynism requires understanding via a double timeline, the one long-term—the increasing intra-party cartelization of the British Labour Party—and one short-term, relating to the fallout of the 2008 credit crisis. In considering these issues, the sense in which Corbynism qualifies as "populist" will also become clearer. On the basic, colloquial level, application of the term "populist" here may seem unwarranted. Applied in an organizational and ideological sense, however, the populist character of Corbynism becomes more understandable. It invoked the older Blairite slogan "The many against the few" and saw itself as representing a forgotten "people" in British politics distinct from the Tory coalition.

The institutional legacy of British cartelization played a sensitive role here. Tony Blair steadily cut ties with what remained of union influence; his commitment to amending Clause IV of the party constitution (defending nationalization) exemplified a broader ideological shift, centralizing power around him inside the party while curtailing parliamentary supremacy in Britain as a whole. As Peter Mair noted, this led to a peculiar adoption of seemingly conflicting ideas across various disparate social groups, in a country whose political culture hardly had such precedents. Blair introduced regional assemblies for Wales and granted Scottish autonomy. Furthermore, although never a supporter of the euro, Blair remained a participant in European unification efforts through the Lisbon and Nice treaties. Central bank independence was one of Blairism's most hallowed goals. With Ed Balls in the Treasury, New Labour saw the Bank of England as a powerful counterforce to inflation thanks to its status as an unelected power. Inviting an increasing number of non-party members into its administration, from experts in "quangos" to spin doctors, Labour engaged in a specifically British cartelization within a bipartisan parliamentary system with a strongly technocratic basis in the civil service.

At the same time, populist elements ran through the New Labour project from the beginning. Rather than going through classic party channels, Blair sought direct connection with electorates and set great store by public relations. He also switched from the older language of "class" to that of the "people," exemplified by his Diana elegy. In the 1990s, modernizers such as Stuart Hall were already urging Labourites to drop this antiquated emphasis on class. Although they had always retained a presence with the party, their arguments began to acquire fresh plausibility in the wake of the Thatcherite offensive of the 1980s. Such a shift also required a different electoral projection. Worried by Labour's lack of support in middle-class sectors, Blair promised less union militancy and more homeownership, consolidating the financialization of the economy ushered in by the Thatcher era. Since working-class voters had "nowhere else to go," Labour retained a broader coalition between newly propertied middle classes and the post-industrial working classes tied to a national welfare state.

The 2008 crisis ripped apart the fractious social contract which had bound this Labour coalition together. Austerity shrunk public sectors across the country, pushing a large part of the domestic working class into destitution. Its impact was also generationally skewed. Younger citizens now faced an economy with declining investment in long-term jobs and mounting precarity. While fighting the central banking crisis saved the financial sector, it also resulted in ushering further rentiership through the back door.

As investments were pulled out of the real economy, capital increasingly flowed into asset-holding and bonds. This pushed up rents in larger cities, where many young Britons ended up after their university studies. The confluence of these factors proved incendiary, driving younger voters into a Labour Party still dedicated to austerity but unable to cater for a new urban electorate. Three main factors explain the internal nature of Corbyn's populist revolt. Unlike the Greek case, the majoritarian aspect of the British electoral system made external party success more difficult. The case of UKIP winning 12.6 percent of the vote in 2015, but only securing one MP, exemplifies the limits of constructing a viable left-wing alternative to Labour in the Commons. In 2013, filmmaker Ken Loach and a group of Socialist Workers Party–affiliated activists tried to field candidates for exactly such an alternative. These options quickly faced a stark electoral ceiling, however, and found it difficult to make inroads in established Labour constituencies. When Corbyn ascended to the position of leader in 2015, the group duly supported Labour again. Here, internal radicalism had solved the problem of an alternative; there were no competing arguments on the left, and no enemies either.

The shape of this challenge was never set in stone, however. Although a powerful driver of the internal revolt, the first-past-the-post system was hardly sufficient to fully explain Corbynism's intraparty nature. As Corbyn himself acknowledged in 2015, a strong second factor was the ideological presence of an Old Labour tradition within Labour itself. In the 1970s, Corbyn had allied with Bennite currents in Labour and strongly opposed EEC membership for the country. Throughout the New Labour years from 1998 to 2010, Corbyn remained a recalcitrant backbencher and defied party whips several times. His commitment to anti-imperialist positions and vocal opposition to the Iraq War distinguished him from mainstream party opinion in the 2000s. Added to the restrictions of first-past-the-post, this maintenance of an alternative tradition within the Labour Party also made intra-party populism a more viable alternative than extra-party intervention.

A final driving factor was a consequence of "latent popularization"— Ed Miliband's opening of the party list to non-members. Miliband introduced American-style primaries to Labour and made it possible for non-members to vote on party leaders, on condition of paying a small fee. This reform radically lowered the threshold for a populist overhaul. In its emphasis on technological innovation and automation, Corbynism received an impetus centered around technical expertise. Yet there also was a strongly organizational legacy on this techno-populist front. The Labour-supporting grass-roots organization Momentum, for instance, combined focused electoral campaigning with digital outreach, in which members could consult online and vote on policy platforms. Such emphases on digital democracy were coupled with discourses celebrating full automation and a new jobless economy. Continuities with Blair's techno-populism went beyond the merely rhetorical, however. Sociologically, Corbynism also seemed to draw from the same wells as the Blairite coalition—an urban precariat and middle class—and inclined to "hyper-urbanism." By bringing in think tanks and cold-shouldering unions, Corbynism combined an appeal to a popular subject with an emphasis on technical expertise and digital democracy. Beyond its personalism ("no Corbynism without Corbyn"), the faction thus saw itself as the representative of a non-class-based majority which could rely on technocratic assistance to realize its principles of social justice.

The new millennials' hybrid status as members also testified to the transformation of the party over the last decades. In the 1950s, Labour was chained to a hinterland of trade unions and workingmen's associations which assured its access to a wider voting pool. Instead of being loyal voters attached to clubs and unions, the new recruits joined as atomized individuals. They were ready to crash the party, yet without the social labels and disciplinary halo usually tied to this membership. More ironically, Miliband's primaries system was originally devised to lower the clout of the unions inside the party. Granting parity to unions and members, he claimed, would enroot Labour back in society and reverse its secular decline.

Although temperamentally on the left compared to his brother, David, Miliband himself had little time for Tony Benn's radical industrial strategies or reshoring. After five years of austerity dictates, MPs had expected the public to lurch leftward. Yet the surge did not materialize—rising house prices and a strategic lock on pensions assured Tory dominance in the home counties, while urban progressives split their votes across Labour and Liberal Democrat MPs. The result was a Labour Party critically weakened, shocked by the evaporation of what had seemed an assured victory.

Corbyn presented a different persona altogether. As a hangover from a previous Bennite wave, he had survived throughout Blair's ice age. After the restructuring of the British economy in the 1990s, he held fast to the industrial strategy of the 1970s. By the middle of the 1980s, it was said that "the option no longer exists." Two factors proved central in preserving Corbyn's independence in the Blairite interregnum. The first was an anti-imperialist legacy that kept him at odds with the American pivot which the Blair cabinet officialized in the early 2000s.

More importantly, Corbyn had latched onto a transformative policy vision which went beyond the private growth plans of the New Labourites dominant since the 1990s. A backbencher with little rhetorical bravado, it was precisely this antihero status that assured Corbyn's survival in the new neoliberal climate. He hibernated and sheltered from the storm, preserved the sacred scrolls, and would step into the breach when required. This implied personnel management and party discipline—two practices he himself had regularly eluded and criticized. The internal Bonapartism installed by Blair both benefited and handicapped the Corbynite insurgents. It gave them a party which was easier to steer from the top; at the same time, it made controlling that party highly dependent on electoral success. This success, in turn, was heavily conditioned by a media atmosphere which tied voting tallies to support from a range of outlets. The party bequeathed by Blair, then, was effective but unstable, hollowed out from the inside but still capable of flexing muscle once it had outside support. It was molded by the void, but also capable of navigating it with great aptitude and extending itself from cycle to cycle.

The new party constructed by Corbyn was similarly a reflection of this volatile environment. As an organization, Momentum was strongly anchored in social media and the wider digital world, and exhibited a clear metropolitan bias. Its generational skew was also beyond doubt. A large contingent of young, educated "networked outsiders" constituted the very core of the cadre and policy team, as well as occupying the informal roles. Yet sociology was not destiny. The first influx of members into Labour proved to be overwhelmingly composed of over-forties from peripheral regions, less beholden to the urban electorate which made up the media cohort of Corbynism. Many came out of the public sector, particularly the National Health Service, with no prior experience of radical politics. They constituted a durable but also distant support base for the project. After an initial leadership challenge from Owen Smith—himself a clear hangover from the Blair years—Corbyn prevailed. Smith's campaign relied on all the classic "authentocratic" cues which were the party's stock-in-trade in the long 1990s, conjuring up imaginary images of a working-class majority now banished from public life. In a changing economic environment, their resonance was muted.

The 2017 election seemed to vindicate the young activists. Holding off a second-referendum pledge, the party promised a lighter version of the Tory Brexit. In many urban wards, this triangulation paid off and kept pro-EU voters in the tent. In improbable places such as Canterbury, Chelsea, and Bristol, the electoral map turned red for the first time in years. At the same time, classical Labourite constituencies stuck with the party. Corbyn's reluctance to adopt an openly pro-Remain position reassured Northern voters. Robbed of her majority, Theresa May was forced into a coalition agreement with fringe politicians of the Northern Irish DUP. The settlement was unprecedented and set a lock on further Brexit plans.

Labour did not "win" the election, of course—unlike what some activists liked to pretend in later reports and reminiscing. Nonetheless, the 2017 result saw the largest increase in vote share for the party in the post-war period and an expanded parliamentary bloc. Underneath these gains, however, a pattern of disjuncture was already clear. Corbynism was tying together two completely disparate blocs.

By trying to be everything to everyone, however, Corbyn's Labour also risked emptying itself out. The very fact that the party had forced May's government into a coalition hinted at a rough road ahead for Brexit plans. But Brexit did not disappear overnight. On the other side of the spectrum, a veritable radicalization was overtaking part of the pro-EU bloc, empowered by persistent Tory infighting, and funneled by an increasingly opaque web of funding bodies. New Labour veterans such as communications director Alastair Campbell and Blair himself were ready to man the guns. Sociologically, however, the fit between Corbynism and the Remain base was more conspicuous. Both relied on a networked, intra-urban caste of professionals which had seen concrete material benefits from EU membership. Being on the younger side, they mainly knew British politics as a torture chamber for fiscal discipline, not as a site for sovereignty. The benefits of the free movement and exchange programs offered by European integration had greater appeal for this constituency than for other working classes, who simply registered a correlation between European integration and declining industrial capacity.

This aversion was not simply cultural. More concretely, many British workers on the bottom rungs of the labor market associated EU membership with the UK's transformation into an employer of last resort for ailing European labor markets, mainly in Southern Europe. The ripple effects were plain to see: Podemos built a London section made up of graduates who had fled Spanish labor markets, while Syriza personnel had often held posts at British universities. Blair and Brown had never pushed Britain into the eurozone, of course, even while facilitating free movement. Given the setup of the UK economy after Thatcher, an influx of cheap European labor could keep the British service economy running. In the 2010s, this partial integration carried risky knock-on effects. After the European Central Bank hiked interest rates in 2011, the eurozone itself plunged into a persistent recession. Job opportunities dwindled. Many European workers migrated to Europe's most open economy, often with skill sets superior to those of its undereducated labor force. The political economy of immigration set a deadlock on the Brexit debate. In fact, the real cause of British low wages lay in overwhelming employer power and low productivity.

These factors further strained Corbyn's positioning in the Brexit proceedings. Temperamentally, he had always belonged to the more Euroskeptic wing of the party. He had seen Europeanization as an alibi for neoliberalization. Yet this did not chime well with other elements of the Corbynite bloc. Given the frail internal ties which the party had built up, coalitioneering proved a difficult exercise. Instead, figures such as John McDonnell, James Meadway, and Keir Starmer were swayed by the wave of popular anti-Brexit anger. They thus postponed any internal debate, and, from Corbyn's point of view, persuasion on the question of "Lexit," or a left-wing exit plan from the European Union. Corbyn found himself caught between loyal advisors and diffuse opinion polling. The latter hinted at the arithmetic danger of letting Remainers take over the party. Even though the "People's Marches" against the Brexit vote in 2019 comprised a demographic tranche hardly amenable to voting Labour, there was a new civil society agitating for repeal of the Brexit referendum result as a whole. The pressure proved insurmountable, even with long-standing party activists. The youthful cast of the protests also made for a natural overlap with the constituency Corbyn appealed to.

On top of this disintegrating force lay the debris left over from the Blair epoch. Given that Corbyn enjoyed a solid mandate from the membership, centrist challenges became riskier. Yet there were still other ways of winkling radicals out of the cockpit. Throughout the Corbyn years, several Third Way Blairites defected or began supporting outside initiatives. Most conspicuous in this exodus was the ill-fated attempt by Labour MP Chuka Umunna to kick-start an "Independent Group," which would contest Labour from the right. Although none of these moves proved electorally consequential, they did exacerbate a climate of hostility which fed into the frontal assault launched by the media. An entire archaeology of Corbyn's career was undertaken, from rental contracts to foreign journeys in the 1990s. Corbynites were right to insist that such hostility from the media was a uniquely daunting challenge. Yet the fact that they were so vulnerable to these attacks also testified to an abiding weakness of the project: forced to wage war on an open field without cavalry, it was inevitable that this would create strategic openings for the enemy. A media party will always be vulnerable to media attacks.

The focus on digital outreach then compounded with an increasing use of think-tank wizardry. Animated by figures such as James Meadway, Ann Pettifor, Joe Guinan, Mariana Mazzucato, Anastasia Nesvetailova, or David Blanchflower, Corbyn's Labour Party saw its proposals to end austerity as part of "economic commonsense" and politically rational. Together with Momentum's reliance on the online and the construction of a "digital party," the specifically technocratic nature of Corbyn's left populism came to the fore.

One of the most persistent stumbling blocks proved to be repeated charges of antisemitism. Even in their pettiness, however, the allegations exposed critical weaknesses in the Corbynite machine, beholden to media cycles and helpless to build a base outside of the usual channels of public opinion. Rather than forging a "counter-society," Corbynism found itself in a constant public whirlwind, tossed on the waves of a hostile sea. There were attempts to create a more positive media circuit, of course, from the rising Novara platforms to *Jacobin*'s online hosting of LabourList updates. Yet these ventures, too, had to contend in an ecology essentially hostile to their principles and often had to defer to established media outlets, with Novara hosts forced to invite speakers from the *Financial Times*.

This led to a particular disjuncture in the public perception of Corbyn. Although the policy platform enjoyed wide support throughout his tenure, ranging from nationalization to welfare plans, his persona remained tainted. This was "leaderism without leadership": complete dependence on a captain whose mastery of the ship was never fully secure.

The calculus proved spectacularly disastrous in the 2019 election. Though Labour pulled in the core metropolitan vote, ex-industrial England deserted the party en masse. The Red Wall narrative had been constructed by Tory spin doctors to divine an unlikely victory. Yet it contained a kernel of truth that even staunch Labour supporters could not deny. Labour had failed to retain Brexit voters in many Northern counties, while its "progressive coalition" around cities proved too frail to draw moderates into the fold. Working classes with their pensions in mind refused Corbyn's calculus of risk, facilitated by decades of diminishing expectations. The swing was abrupt: classic mining towns went blue for the first time, as traditional Labour voters stayed home or switched rolls. McDonnell and the soft Remainers stood exposed. Corbyn ultimately failed to bridge the gap between a metropolitan middle class, squeezed by the rentier economy, and a post-industrial working class abandoned by British capital decades ago. This was always a difficult cohabitation. Welding together these two blocs had proved too difficult, the more so for a party long since denatured by Blairism.

It's Our Party Now: The Sanders Campaign

Voters lined up by the thousands. The coup de grâce had finally been delivered: Bernard Sanders had lost his second bid for the American presidency. Four months before, the scene had looked vastly different: newspapers were running op-eds on the fact that Sanders had "captured" the party, leading socialists to proclaim that "it's our party now." In their attempt to kidnap the institution, though, they had in fact already failed; as insurgents, they were left standing at the gates.

Like Corbyn, Sanders had weathered the neoliberal ice age with a unique set of tools. Born to Brooklyn immigrants, Sanders studied at Chicago and found his way into state politics. As a mayor in Vermont, he tried to build a small outpost of social democracy. In the 1990s, he grabbed a Senate seat and became known as a talented cross-partisan broker. He worked with John McCain on veteran welfare and, like Corbyn, was a staunch opponent of imperial adventurism in the 2000s. In a country with a critically weak socialist tradition, holding this position was no easy feat. Burlington-born radicalism had to face hostile federal laws and an underdeveloped welfare state. More dangerously, it forced Sanders to become a hesitant fellow traveler of the Democrats' left wing, a former "party of workers" which had never, in fact, been a workers' party.

This dragged American politics into a protracted time loop, punctuated by two periods of intense campaigning. By 2019, Sanders was ready to make a second run for the presidency. This campaign yielded a surprising parallel with his previous bid: overperforming in Western states, coming up against a hard wall in the South. Once again, he was a lone progressive figure among a broadly conservative set. There were some subtle differences this time, however. In 2016, an unprecedented space had opened up on the left after Elizabeth Warren declined to run. Throughout that season, memories of the 1963 March on Washington and sit-ins at Chicago were a constant. These gelled with the sensibilities of a younger generation knocked sideways by the 2008 credit crash. Not only did they inhabit a society with an underdeveloped welfare state, the fallout of the 2008 crisis had been quite different from the economic disarray that had inspired other populist challengers in the past. A party state made third-party challenges much more difficult now, in the twenty-first century. Instead of fielding outsider candidates, the idea would be to capture an established party infrastructure and wield it to different ends, potentially moving the entire field leftward. Decapitation of a leadership structure or displacement of an existing party was implausible at best. A pragmatist at heart, Sanders always placed his bets on the Democratic ticket as a safer launch pad for his political aims.

The contrast with the Trump insurgency proved instructive. Unconstrained by fealty to a GOP establishment, Trumpites were able to crash the party and use it as a tool for personal enrichment, without, at first, any clear prospects for victory. Once it was clear that established candidates would bite the dust, Trump was able to extend his patrimonial business empire into his political office, collapsing the line between public and private. Sanders was in no position to undertake this maneuver—there was no crashing or displacing any party. In its own way the Sanders campaign was a creature of this post-2008 environment. Like Corbyn, Sanders had survived the unipolar 1990s on a local level, keeping the politics of the Democratic machine at bay. Yet there was a clear symbiosis between both institutions, too: Bernie had consistently voted and collaborated with politicians from both parties and had a concrete policy record. Although personally popular, Barack Obama left the Democratic Party in a state of profound disarray. TARP had reinflated corporate balance sheets but led to a dearth of public investment. The result was a squeezed middle class and an evisceration of working-class savings across the bottom of the labor market. The politics of symbolism had to substitute for an economic policy agenda, whether addressing police violence or public healthcare initiatives.

More than a pop-up campaign, Sanders' ambitions remained deeply DIY. Without any organic ties to the DNC establishment, he had to engineer his own campaign machine. This proved both a handicap and a boon to his electoral efforts. On the one hand, it allowed Sanders to distance himself from the donor class which kept a lock on radical bids within the Democratic Party. He was not tainted by association with the Rubinite consensus. On the other, it required constant cash injections from an individualized base. In states where such an electorate was held in firmer control by the Democratic machine, reaching out to voters would prove a far more demanding exercise. Their loyalty to local Democratic politicians, in a particular form of ethnic cartelization, was beyond question. If they had even heard of him in the first place, Sanders struck them as a risk rather than an opportunity: likely to inflame GOP revanchism with his redistributive plans, and unreliable in his commitment to voting rights in remoter states. How could Sanders bring this constituency into the fold?

Sanders's bid also required a new financial strategy. Rather than rely on the Super PAC system, the idea was to raise individual donations. On one occasion, a Sanders rally was interrupted by a Black Lives Matter activist who criticized the senator for his supposed silence on racial questions. The majority Sanders sought to gather had to cut across these lines. On the one hand, he had to bring along a provincial working class left behind by deindustrialization. These voters would team up with a new class of service workers in inner cities, plagued by rising rents and falling wages, more ethnically diverse and tied to the politics of urban progressivism. The fit between these two groups, as with Corbynism, was never organic. Inevitably, this geography had to spread outward too, pulling in suburbanites who formed a key part of the Democratic demographic. Here the question became much thornier, however.

A presidential system not only kneecaps possible third-party challengers. It also locks in a particularly exhausting campaign cycle. After the Trump victory, Sanders decided to focus on legislative work and join the broader anti-Trump coalition. This pact proved as risky as it was necessary. On the one hand, it forced Sanders into cohabitation with the very establishment figures he once set out to displace, now joined by luminaries from the national security domain, responsible for the Middle Eastern wars he had opposed. On the other, it provided a necessary buffer to an ever more insurgent hard right, willing to ride roughshod over the Constitution and obstruct the peaceful transfer of power. Increasingly militant in outlook, the GOP now sought to muster a hard-right, antimajoritarian strategy to secure its hold over the American state apparatus. Against contenders of this caliber, even outsiders like Sanders preferred to be safe rather than sorry.

A tumultuous intermission between two presidential runs, the Trump years nonetheless proved to be a difficult test of endurance for the Sanders camp. Through sheer exigency, these years pushed Sanders closer to the center of the party. The outsider status which Sanders had carefully maintained throughout the Clinton era was collapsing into an uneasy halfway position. The repeated impeachment trials, combined with the persistence of Russiagate, made many of Sanders's stances indistinguishable from those of the Democratic mainstream.

All of this preceded the campaign's march into the South. There, Democratic loyalty, especially among black voters, would present a stubborn problem for the Sanders insurgency. While in the North the legacy of Clintonite deindustrialization and welfare reform soaked a group of disaffiliated voters from the Democratic bloc, the South retained a much sturdier party infrastructure. Now more than ever, the results of the Southern strategy kept Democratic voters in a state of loyal isolation. Their expectations had been diminishing for years. Already in 2016, they had stuck with Hillary Clinton out of loyalty, rather than crossing over to the challenger. Despite the material trials of the Obama years, the risk analysis of these voters was a great deal more pessimistic than that of the urban millennials who had fielded Sanders in other races. In 2020, these limits crystallized into an even harder wall. Despite Joe Biden's instrumental role in the welfare and crime reforms of the 1990s, which had sent millions of black voters behind bars, the seeming emergency of the Trump years had sucked oxygen out of the space opened by 2016.

There were, however, some victories during that time which Sanders supporters could point to—from the entry of the "Squad" into Congress, to left-wing pressure on the Biden administration's COVID response. All in all, however, Sanders's presence in the 2020 primaries felt strangely disarticulated: he had whetted an appetite for radicalism among a section of the American electorate while exposing the irrationality of America's political economy. Yet he had no party to work with, or campaign infrastructure which could survive through the next cycle. Meanwhile the protests spawned by the George Floyd killing radically abrogated the strategy Sanders had planned. Again, the void filled by forty years of machine politics proved all too difficult to navigate. By May 2020, with the world paralyzed by lockdowns, Sanders had transitioned back into the role of extra-party broker he had played for decades. Behind him he left a new but fragmented landscape of think tanks, podcasts, and congressional committees, which could pressure without providing heft. Like its

European counterparts, American left populism had already
exhausted itself.

The COVID shutdowns accelerated a demobilization already
underway in several populist quarters. As Sanders retreated
to the Senate and Corbyn to the Commons, Podemos readied itself for government and La France insoumise prepared
for its upcoming election. In public appearances, references
to Mouffe and Laclau's work became increasingly scarce. In
Latin America, the United States, and Europe, the populist
momentum seemed to have run out of steam. Across these
cases, a more classical left–right cleavage had reimposed itself
after the populist intermission.

In the resultant tumult there had been painfully little time
for reflection. What exactly was the populist-left balance sheet?
Where did it succeed, where did it fail, and was it in any way
likely to be repeated? For some cases a diagnosis was objec-
tively clear, from a real participation in government (Podemos)
to total electoral rout (Corbyn's Labour, Syriza), while for
others the legacy was charged with ambivalence (La France
insoumise, Sanders). Any assessment of the left's populist
gamble was also intimately tied to its capacity to face up to
the two dilemmas of twenty-first-century left politics—the
social content of its coalition and its new organizational form.

The peculiarity of the setup and background conditions
only renders this assessment more difficult. Like any club,
the populists had to contend with a shifting professional
and commercial environment. The "void" of party politics
opened by the crisis reforms of the 1970s compounded with the

divergent trajectories following the 2008 credit crash. Inevitably, the economic crisis combined with a crisis of politics *itself*: Overweening leader-figures presided over the tightly organized mass parties of yore, while voters and supporters could be drawn only on a temporary basis. In the post-political age, the demands made on star players were increasingly stringent and supporters became more difficult to draw in. Any postgame analysis should focus on the three components of this populist moment—the captain, the tactics, and the crowd, and how each chose to rise to the specific challenges thrown up by the "long 2010s."

4.

POPULIST POSTGAME

In 1984, the English rock musician Robert Wyatt released a song in defense of the British miners' strike. The track had a lengthy genesis. Having achieved renown with the cult band Soft Machine, Wyatt underwent a public radicalization in the late 1970s, highlighted by his membership of the Communist Party of Great Britain and appearances on various trade-union picket lines. A similar radicalism was detectable in his 1984 four-track EP, *The Age of Self*, co-produced with the Grimethorpe Colliery Brass Band and the embattled trade unionists of Britain's GCHQ intelligence unit. Wyatt's track was a fierce indictment of Thatcherism and its gospel of egoism, coupled with a sensitive critique of recent trends in left-wing thought. The song opened with the following lines:

> They say the working class is dead, we're all consumers now
> They say that we have moved ahead, we're all just
>   people now
> They say we need new images to help our movement grow
> They say that life is broader based, as if we didn't know

The targets of Wyatt's invective were clear. Code words such as "consumers," "people," and "images" stood out as angry retorts to recent calls from within the Labour Party to remodel it as a broad, "popular" coalition, capable of taking on the Thatcherite camp. After the latter achieved its first general election victory in 1979, figures such as Neil Kinnock and Peter Mandelson argued for Labourites to reorient themselves around a larger middle-class base and reach out to "common," rather than "working," people. As with Eric Hobsbawm's speech on the "The Forward March of Labour Halted," a populist sensibility was in the air.[1]

The cultural theorist Stuart Hall was perhaps the subtlest adherent to Kinnock's turn. Hall's work in *Marxism Today* on the "Great Moving Right Show" in the late 1970s had put the case for a "democratic populism" against Thatcher's "authoritarian" variant. Although a dedicated socialist, Hall had an uneasy relationship with the mainstream labor movement. In his view, the miners' strike was "doomed to be fought and lost as an old rather than as a new form of politics." Although its goal "instinctually lay with the politics of the new"—visible in the miners' alliance with feminist and gay rights groups—the strike was "fought and lost" precisely because of Labour's "imprisonment in the categories and strategies of the past."[2]

The early 1990s seemed to bring much-needed relief. In the early years of the decade, Hall saw an opening in the ascension of Tony Blair, who was determined to bury the party's "hard left." Hall's enthusiasm cooled markedly in the course of the 1990s; he now came to see Blairism as "The Great Moving Nowhere Show." Blair's populism, Hall realized, had merely served as a device for the neoliberal rewiring of Britain—the privatization of rail services, release of central bankers from political pressure, and remodeling of social services toward a customer-based model. As Hall saw it, the neoliberal makeover was only sugarcoated with some multicultural topping.

Thirty years after the crushing of the miners' strike, left populists inherited an even fiercer version of Hall's dilemma. What did a trade of the "working class" for the "people" mean for Europe's left populists? As the 2010s drew to a close, the authors asked Spanish activists to reflect on that decade. Asked about their militancy, activists and ex-activists spoke of politics in the past tense: a profound sense of disappointment, tinged with a certain nostalgia. For those who had been active in a movement from the start, who had seen a newborn party take shape and grow, the feeling of disenchantment verged on the depressive. They had ridden a great, powerful tide of hope and gazed at the future from its crest; they had felt as if they were regaining control over their lives; they had developed a sense of belonging to something bigger than themselves; they had glimpsed a possible victory. Even more painfully, camaraderie between populists had given way to personal enmity, acrimony, even hatred between former teammates. At the end of the political cycle opened by the Great Recession, they were feeling—and looked—considerably older. They had aged, but time had also sped up. Flying out of the whirlwind several years on, they touched their faces and found wrinkles.

This did not mean that their balance sheet was negligible. In the 2010s, left populists had proven capable of hijacking big electoral machines, conquering national governments from both majority and minority positions, and winning several municipal seats in the cities. The forces in question had drawn lessons from the two modes of politics which had dominated the last twenty years: PR and protest. For the former, they rewired the communication and media skills honed by increasingly cartel-like parties during the neoliberal ice age. For the latter, they drew on the horizontal participation introduced by the occupations of the squares and other protest movements. They developed an earnest interest in power, for they did not believe one could "change the world without taking it." They were serious about reorganizing into parties, but were also closely bound to a world in which the power of the parties had structurally weakened. They thus tailored a type of radical politics perfectly adapted to the environment created by the 2008 credit crash. Overall, they showed that "an" alternative was possible, while exercising a lasting influence on the mainstream political agenda—either directly, by governing at the national and local level, or less directly, by by putting pressure on mainstream parties.

In retrospect, however, expectations and reality were severely mismatched. Several left-populist activists were left with a sense of wasted opportunity. Particularly since, as chapter 2 made clear, all the conditions for a breakthrough had been met: shrinking loyalty to—and diminished credibility of—traditional parties across the board, along with the sudden appearance of powerful social movements, fresh policy platforms, and capable leaders; a favorable set of circumstances by any standards. If the left was incapable of crushing competitors in this environment, what would happen in less propitious conditions? As a former cadre member of Podemos confessed in an informal talk in July 2019, it felt as if the party had lost while playing on the best possible terrain. It was like playing a first-leg game before a crowd of supporters with a one-man advantage and obliging referee—only to end on a draw.

The activists also pointed to deeper constraints on their enterprise. Brexit proved an intractable obstacle to Britain's left-populist venture and its effort to bring together the middle-class, well-educated constituency of urban centers with working classes in the industrial and deindustrialized regions. Similarly, Podemos was particularly uncomfortable with the Catalan issue, which became too salient to be ignored and too divisive for its electorate. And, of course, the financial rain of blows to which Greek populists were subjected knocked them out almost immediately. Leaving aside the peculiarities of each of these national cases, the wider backdrop against which all these parties operated became visible. Here, the left-populist contenders followed a distinct pattern: an impressive upsurge, based on innovative methods and leading to resounding electoral successes, then electoral stagnation and strategic hesitation, provoking harsh internal tensions. This pattern calls for thorough, structural explanations. Why did left populists systematically run into both regional and European walls? Why was it so difficult for contenders to sustain their performance beyond the political honeymoon? Why did populist activists tear each other to pieces when faced with the first setbacks? And why did it prove so difficult for each of these parties to properly institutionalize and bind voters to them?

A certain paradox stalked each contender here. By and large, the very environment that enabled the parties in question to gain a foothold also proved profoundly disabling to them in the long term. The shared fate of these left populists also indicates how their strategy affected their environment. The populist left is a political species particularly capable of adapting to the new "ecosystem" of an unmediated democracy. Its malleability allows it to attract voters beyond traditional class-based alignments; its emphasis on the leader as the unifying figure for the movement suits the personalization of contemporary politics; its communication strategies enable it to attract young voters through social media; its antiestablishment attitude helps it capture the strong sentiment against the elites that has flourished since 2008. This ecosystem, however, contains one major risk factor—the void is either *not empty enough* or *too empty altogether*. Left populists had to work within structures of mediation that had undeniably been eroded yet had not wholly disappeared—two factors which proved particularly bothersome to the populist left. The decomposition of traditional parties, trade unions, churches, and civic organizations—as well as of the broader social group they stood for—had not been fully accomplished. In fact, the resilience of these structures varied from one country to another, imposing a different set of constraints on each of these left-populist actors. The void thus left them in a double bind. Where the disintegration of party democracy is too advanced, the extreme atomization of the electorate dangerously increases the volatility of the political game. It also makes it harder for populist actors to permanently lash voters and members to their mast. Where this disintegration is *less* advanced, the competitive advantage of traditional parties and the residual loyalty of specific social groups impose severe limits on populism's capacity to build a cross-class coalition of its own. In sum, populists found themselves between a rock and a hard place.

A series of questions ensued. Should left populism seek alliances with surviving center-left parties and consolidate its gains, albeit at the risk of ceding outsider status? Or should it stick to its mostly digital, pop-up-style organization to launch blitzkrieg campaigns across election cycles? Alternatively, should it design a sturdier party structure, fit to wage trench warfare over years? And once it has successfully entered the arena of electoral politics, should it relocate itself more clearly along the left–right axis, or preserve its ideological indeterminacy? These questions are not simply organizational.

Each left-populist outfit faced its own version of these dilemmas. And in each case, despite a favorable scenario at the kickoff, the upshot was a draw in the first leg. As with any team, left populism's fate is intimately linked to the relationship it shapes between the individuals and the collective, to its tactics on the pitch, and to the structure—both financial and social—of the club itself. The coming pages scrutinize how the populist left has tried to navigate its partially empty space, by successively passing through each of these layers: how it handled the relation between the team and its star player, how it relied on digital tactics to bond with its supporters, and how it managed and tended the club itself.

The Populist Captain

Any participant in a team sport is familiar with the argument
that in the absence of a collective strategy it is better to pass
the ball to a star player. Every culture has its own term for this
participant: "crack player," "*fuoriclasse*," "*estrella*," incarnated
by figures such as Bobby Charlton, Roberto Baggio, Diego
Armando Maradona. In modern soccer, it is not unusual to
see the star player becoming even more important than the
team—in terms of financial weight, reputational capital, and
sporting performance—to the extent that Cristiano Ronaldo,
Lionel Messi, or Neymar Junior can represent a bigger brand
than the club they play for. On the pitch, they provide alternative strategies: against a well-oiled collective machine, their
individual exploits can force the best defensive locks. Often,
it's not about their technical skills or physical abilities alone:
their mere *presence* intimidates opponents, who are cowed by
their almost mystical aura. They play the role of strong, charismatic leaders for clubs that find it hard to survive on their own.

The role of populist leader bears a striking resemblance to
these athletic figures. Given the disorganization of the "people,"
it comes as no surprise that contemporary left populism has
consistently gambled on this type of strategy. For years, the
radical left had lived with the idea that participation in elections
was more important than winning them. After all, weren't the
elections themselves a product of the "society of the spectacle"
any truly anticapitalist force should aim to resist? Wasn't the
whole show strongly biased in favor of liberal and reactionary forces? In these conditions, the radical left often agreed

to play a small part on election day—hoping at least to win a little visibility and get a couple of issues on the floor—and focused instead on the creation of spaces uncontaminated by capitalist logic, such as temporary autonomous zones. Against the neoliberal order, exodus was an attractive motto. From this angle, the left could afford a relatively lackluster organizational set up, as it did not need to appear as a credible force of governance. Nor did it have to hold together a large, diverse coalition of social groups—only purists and militants could remain inside the club. For any political force truly eager to deploy a counter-hegemonic strategy, however, the question of leadership cannot be avoided. Vying for power requires, at the minimum, the capability of playing with loaded dice.

In the media, the personality-driven mood of today's politics makes it almost impossible to win elections without the asset of a recognizable leader. Personal qualities trump all else in the modern political battleground. Sanders and Corbyn could claim moral incorruptibility; Iglesias and Mélenchon deployed outstanding oratory skills; Tsipras could package his pragmatic ethos with a youthful and telegenic vigor. Except for Syriza's leader, none of them based their notoriety on an older party career—and, even in the Greek case, the power relation between the leader and his political formation quickly reversed, as Syriza became more and more dependent on its figurehead to appear as a credible force of government. Podemos was similar: Iglesias was *literally* the face of the purple party when it was created out of the blue. Mélenchon's notoriety largely exceeded that of the successive platforms he created after he left the Socialist Party (Parti de Gauche, France insoumise, Union

Populaire). He had almost always been a minority figure within the center-left formation—to the extent that several observers, after the 2022 legislative elections, ironically commented on his cannibalizing the leftovers of the Socialist Party from the outside, describing this move as his first victory in a social-ist convention. As for old-timers Sanders and Corbyn, both drew their legitimacy from their statuses as quixotic, self-proclaimed "socialist" legislators (an especially rare species in the US political ecosystem). Sanders was entirely independent from big party machines, while Corbyn could boast about his lasting commitment to the margins of his party—a truly leftist Labourite who had never caught the Blairite bug.

In the streets too, a strong leader was indispensable for tying together such diverse coalitions. After thirty years of neoliberal restructuring, the social movements had slowly faded away. More importantly, they had been thoroughly disorganized. The activists who first occupied the squares did not look much like the old protesters of the twentieth century—the men and women who'd been organized and disciplined by trade unions, political parties, and civic organizations. In the 2010s, this kind of unity and discipline was in short supply—it would have to be built from the ground up. The antiausterity coalitions were quite disparate—the lost generation, a squeezed middle class, and the new precarious poor—and most of them, unlike the former industrial working class, lacked an older tradition of social mobilization to call upon. In fact, many people on the squares were first-timers, while for some, it was their very first experience of speaking in public. All these groups, who were otherwise at risk of drifting apart, certainly found a common inspiration in the calls for democracy and renewed popular sovereignty. Any institutional translation of their demands, however, would require a much stronger glue to hold them together, especially considering that a winning strategy would have to include the working class of the industrial and post-industrial areas.

Yet that inclusion would not be easy. Since the publication of the infamous Terra Nova Report—compiled by a think tank close to the French Socialist Party in 2011—the goal of uniting the working class with the urbanized middle class had become like squaring a circle. In an atomized landscape of this kind, the presence of a leader capable of aggregating the demands and channeling them in public space becomes even more important. As a matter of fact, the role of the leader is one of the most central—and controversial—elements in Ernesto Laclau's theory of populism: the more the "chain" of demands is heterogeneous and extended—as is most often the case in modern politics, with a multitude of demands related to economic, gender, racial, and environmental issues—the less its unity can be taken for granted. The figure of the leader "condenses" the unity of the crowd and provides it with a magnet for affective investment. Representation here turns into *embodiment*: the leader is the people, and the people is the leader. As Hugo Chávez famously said: "I am not myself anymore, I am a people."

The populist left thus gave in wholesale to the "hyperleaderism" of our era. Rather than a universal trait of populism as such (although populism has notorious affinities with charismatic leaders, there are examples of leaderless populism throughout history), the prominence of the leader appears as a defining feature of today's politics, a necessary response to both social dispersion and media centrality. Hyperleaders draw their legitimacy from the "emotional recognition and acclaim of the base,"[3] rather than from a legal investiture by the party machine. In fact, their role is often predicated on the rejection of party bureaucracy; they act as a sort of "ultimate mediator" who renders the other layers of mediation obsolete. The necessary traits of the hyperleader are almost always the same: media-savvy, predicated on an image of authenticity and honesty, displaying a down-to-earth attitude, presenting as the spokesperson of the movement rather than its head.[4] As the leader turns into a point of projection for the "followers," the relation between the base and the party—both in organizational and ideological terms—becomes secondary, at best. "Corbynism," "Mélenchonisme," and "Pablismo" signal the direct bond between the leader and the crowd which enables them to bypass the construction of a common home. While those signifiers might seem reminiscent of the left's tendency toward the cult of personality, they could not, in fact, be more distinct from ancestors such as "Leninism," "Stalinism," "Trotskyism," or "Maoism." Those were the names of specific branches of a common faith, particular interpretations of a shared ideological corpus. Rather than pointing to the abilities of a star player bringing victory to a disorganized team, they implied a totalizing philosophy of play.

Its leaderism is likely one of the features that make populism so well equipped for the personalized, unmediated, and digitalized cast of today's politics. Its downside is less visible. In fact, critics see the populist left as living in the perpetual shadow of a Caesarist derailing, not to say an authoritarian turn. While this fear is probably exaggerated—and deliberately raised by liberals to discredit any energetic challenge to the hegemonic bloc—the payoffs of this leader-centrism are not always clear, indeed they are sometimes outweighed by its limitations. It gives the illusion that the leader's unique skills, visibility, and voluntarism could suffice to herd older blue-collar workers back to the left and knot them together with the younger, middle-class voters of urban districts.

That coalition never materialized. Podemos barely managed to get a foothold outside the urban areas—it failed to attract voters from the "emptied Spain" (*España vaciada*), those large territories drained of their population by the massive rural exodus of the post-war years. Mélenchon, at the height of his electoral performance in April 2022, had still not convinced the "angry but not fascist" to vote for him—in fact, his electoral bastions were all located in the most urbanized parts of the country (the highly educated youth and the suburban proletariat of the service sector) while he still lagged behind the far right in the historically (post-)industrial areas, where abstention prevails. As for Corbyn, the precarious coalition he attempted to forge between blue-collar Northern workers and cosmopolitan Southern millennials dissolved over the Brexit vote. In this regard, left populism largely failed to deliver on its promises. The prominent role of the leader, useful as it can sometimes be, essentially works as a way of camouflaging the unresolved issues that hamper the left's performances (disorganization and atomization of civil society, emptying out of the national level of decision-making, extinction of alternative horizons to the capitalist mode of production, and so on).

Leader-centrism is more than a harmless preference, however. Leaders do not merely impose organizational unity on a populist coalition by tying together a disparate set of demands; they also function as agents who impart ideological coherence to such coalitions in the first place, and overdetermine their life cycles. This, in turn, implies a wholly different set of dependencies between base and leadership, and tends to invert the relationship between the politician and the party. In some cases, the movement's viability itself seems inconceivable without its leader. This dependency is manifest in a question no one in LFI seems capable of answering: Would the movement still exist without Mélenchon? Similarly, one may wonder if there is anything left of Corbynism after the fall of its champion. Crucially, this exacerbated dependence of a movement on its leader can easily turn into a fatal weakness. The more it delegates to a star player, the more a team will collectively suffer from his injuries. When the identification with a down-to-earth, (supposedly) morally irreproachable figure is the prime glue holding a political force together, that figure becomes a sitting duck for any adversaries who—by accusing Corbyn of antisemitism, by pointing at Mélenchon's short temper or Iglesias's expensive tastes—can smear the left-populist camp as a whole. The old-fashioned mass parties on the left had at least one great virtue: an internal *ruling class* ready to assume leadership should the party ever have its head abruptly cut off.

More importantly, leaderism often was more of a symptom than a cure. Rather than mere logistical expediency, populism's dependence on the leader might even testify "precisely to the lack, the weakness, of the social movement of which the leader is the supposed avatar."[5] It must be remembered that the very genesis of Podemos was the *fading away* of the Indignados movement. Podemos's strategy, however, did not aim to lend a perennial afterlife to this wave of mobilization, but rather to harness its residual energy in order to build an electoral machine. When Vistalegre I sanctioned the victory of this vertical strategy against the horizontal, pro–social movement approach advocated by the *"anticapis,"* it was justified by the narrowness of the political window of opportunity the 15-M had opened. In other words, the haste in giving the social upsurge an electoral translation was predicated upon the absolute certainty of its temporary nature and the impossibility of keeping it alive. If the electoral gamble fails, however, there is nothing left to fall back on. When Podemos realized its mistake, it was too late: the wave of mobilization had completely receded, its local circles were moribund, and its intellectual life atrophied. As a last resort, it attached itself to the activist networks of Izquierda Unida, thus embracing the very flaws of left activism it purported to correct: the tendency to confinement within a closed and self-referential universe exclusively composed of dogmatic, older, long-time militants. By the same token, LFI resigned itself to a form of organization able to expand and welcome newcomers in the context of a presidential election, but incapable of developing lasting loyalties in the long run.

The hyperleader, therefore, replaces the fading mediation

without revitalizing it—in fact, accentuating the move to disintermediation. By concentrating all energies on the media performance of its figurehead, left populism readily falls into the traps of clicktivism and gesture politics. It neglects the necessary establishment of a strong horizontal substructure, and ends up exacerbating the undermining of social bonds already fragilized by several decades of neoliberal regime. Moreover, without the extended network of traditional parties which made the party's top executives receptive to social dynamics, left populism must rely on professional "feelers" or "sensors." These left-wing PR wizards are supposed to identify an electorate's "common sense" and extrapolate topics that will win votes. But what if the "feelers" can't feel it? In 2017, a police search at LFI's headquarters spurred its leader into a single-handed crusade against "lawfare" that would elicit nearly no support from other parties, media outfits, unions, or associations. If Mélenchon proclaimed that "he was the Republic," the Republic clearly did not see itself as him. In the absence of collective guardrails, the leader's belief in his own talents can easily turn into personal hubris. Overall, then, the payoffs of the leader-centric approach barely compensate for its negative effects. In the case of left populism, this consecration of the star player considerably affects the relation to the supporters (the populist crowd) and the structure of the club (the populist media).

The Populist Tactic

On April 6, 2022, the French politician Jean-Luc Mélenchon appeared on stage at a rally in Paris. Or rather, Mélenchon himself did not appear: instead, an immaterial image of the French party leader was beamed onto the stage, after which the audience in several cities listened to a speech from the ether. As with his run five years before, Mélenchon had decided to appear as a hologram rather than in the flesh, allowing outreach to a wider circle of sympathizers.

Mélenchon's stunt nodded to an essential feature of the left populist experience in general —its newly digital dimension. This shift not only changed the fundamentals of membership in the organizations in question, in which the line between members and non-members became more diffuse. It also radically altered the dynamics of campaigning, vote-bidding, and base-building upon which left parties had classically relied. As a social form, the internet was still relatively new when the protest waves of the 2008 crisis took off, for all the Arab Spring's baptism as the first "Facebook revolution." By the mid-2010s, however, it had already acquired maturity as a social form and was being used by forces across the spectrum.

The preconditions for this approach were also clear. The extreme marketization of society that defined the 1980s and 1990s made the West uniquely vulnerable to the perils of social media. The disbanding of voluntary organizations, the decline of Fordist job stability (and with it, mass trade unionism), the dwindling of religious life, the evaporation of amateur athletic associations, the "dissolution of the masses" and the rise of a multitudinous crowd of "individuals"—all were forces that generated a demand for social media long before there existed a product like Facebook to supply the consumer. Social media could only grow in a void not of its own making. Social media was thus both an expression of the crisis of the social that predates the internet and a potent accelerator of that crisis. In the first sense, the internet has simply exacerbated the pre-existing trends of the neoliberal period. But at the same time, the internet is not solely a means of communication. It *is* a social form—a type of association or community, or a machine to generate "imagined communities." Any sociologist and philosopher will tell you that we can't separate those two components, of course, and that every new means of communication will spawn its own communities (of reading, say, or the "imagined communities" which historian Benedict Anderson saw as central to his "print capitalism").

Instead, the turn to the digital could also be understood within the frame of the crisis of civil society which the political scientist Peter Mair called the "void." On the one hand, the online thrives off the atomization inflicted on society by the neoliberal offensive in the 1980s and 1990s. More and more, it has become the substitute association for a world in which all associative units have been eroded. (There is ample research showing strong correlations between declining civic commitment and broadband access.) At the same time, the internet accelerates and even entrenches this atomization. In this sense it is hardly a substitute for the older types of civic association we knew from the twentieth century. The exit and entry costs online of our new, simulated civil society are extremely low.

The internet is the ideal exit option for a general "exit society"—allowing people to make their "voice" heard, in Albert Hirschman's sense, while always keeping open the possibility for citizens to drop out and check out. The stigma that comes with leaving a Facebook group or a Twitter subculture is minor compared to having to move out of a neighborhood because you scabbed during a strike. The internet did generate communities, of course, from meme groups to cookery sites. Yet the thickness and density of previous associations—to call them "voluntary" seemed misleading—was nowhere to be found online.

This porousness complicated any left-populist use of digital media. In many ways, the online environment proved a thankfully cheap way of mobilizing interest and drawing in supporters. But cheap entry costs translated into cheap exits. The 100,000 who joined Momentum had little but online mailing lists and Twitter accounts to sign up for; the voting mechanisms by which they exercised power were notoriously opaque. The same held for the email lists from which members of La France insoumise vanished unexpectedly—unsubscribing was an easier way to disaffiliate than relocating from a red municipality. In the case of Podemos, the online portals could not hide the party's reliance on an older cadre of activists, a mainstay of radical left outfits since the 2000s.

Populism's digital parties clearly sought to remedy the top-down dynamics of the mass party model. Yet digitization brought with it its own hierarchies, like the informal appropriation by select figureheads who ran the media debates. In Corbyn's case, this meant that the lines between the inside and outside of the party were increasingly blurred. Anything resembling democratic centralism—in which internal party matters would first be decided in closed circles and a tight party line would be maintained externally—was a distant dream for this approach. Instead, from Bernie-boosting professional posters to the digital crowd behind Mélenchon, many left-populist questions ended up being discussed somewhere between party and public sphere, with the two often bleeding into each other.

The Populist Crowd

"Against Modernization" is hardly the worst slogan for old-style left parties. Much like the "ultra" faction of hardline soccer fans, many activists of these parties would rather lose the next twenty elections than give up on their community, values, and rituals. When life-long communist militants brought their red flags to a demonstration, a Proustian feeling overcame them. They naturally observed the new digital activism, "gaseous" movements, and "beyond left and right" slogans with a sense of deep suspicion: even if they admitted that such novelties might bring visibility and resources to their club and greatly increase its chances of winning, they would never trade their certainties for those possibilities. They would keep on supporting their home club regardless of its performance (*al di là del risultato*, or "regardless of the result," as the famous slogan by SSC Napoli's ultras put it).

Through the transformation of European party politics in the last thirty years, a striking parallel to the structural metamorphosis of the European soccer landscape emerges. Due to the sector's growing commodification, clubs have become less and less dependent on their core fans, both financially and symbolically. Much as a steady stream of funding has driven the cartelization of political parties, the booming business of television rights has revolutionized the political economy of soccer clubs. It empowered a colluding elite whose main interest lies in preventing intruders from diminishing their market share: the Premier League. The old, loyal fans of local origin now began to look like gatecrashers, hampering the expansion of the club's audience with their rowdiness and, in some cases, their hooliganism. The solution proved remarkably easy: overpriced tickets and restricted preferential access to the stadium. Soon the stands of the clubs in question would be filled by a new crowd—less local, and so with a far less passionate investment in the game. The atmosphere in the stadiums began to cool. Dizzying flows of money enabled the clubs to attract the best players in the world and stay competitive at the highest level. The question arose whether they even needed the unruly fans of the past.

Since the neoliberal ice age of the 1990s, most Western political parties have faced a similar temptation. The increasing fluidity of the electoral marketplace makes a catch-all strategy appealing: Why stick to the traditional fanbase when there are plenty of new potential supporters out there, not yet affiliated to a competitor? To attract them, they first lowered the barriers to entry—contrary to football clubs, indeed, here the best way to dilute the influence of old members is to slash prices rather than raise them. No need to pay a membership fee, undergo political vetting and training, or participate in endless meetings.

Instead, the cheap new exit and entry costs meant members could simply *click* their way in and out.

This also implies a clear shift in the commercial ethics of the political club. Access to the "stadium" is no longer restricted to *members* : anyone is one click away from registering, starting an "action group," and campaigning for the party candidate. Nostalgic types might find little to appreciate about this change. Yet it remains an undeniably effective strategy within the void. In a context of flagging political allegiances, increasingly fluid party systems and weaker internal discipline, it provides the populist left (or any new political contender) with an agile electoral vehicle, free from bureaucratic burdens. The method is intended to be extremely cost-effective—cheap and quick politics. It allows politicians to create ad-hoc battle machines custom-built for the conquest of executive power at the national level in record time, based on a minimal set of principles to which people can sign up easily. Such was the ambition of Sahra Wagenknecht when she left Die Linke and founded Aufstehen (Get Up), following the lead of her French neighbor Jean-Luc Mélenchon. The trick is now being performed across the political spectrum: on the left (La France insoumise), by liberals or the radical center (La République en Marche, Italia Viva), or by "non-ideological" forms of populism (Movimento Cinque Stelle, Pirate Party). Those electoral machines celebrate their distance from the traditional political families, right down to their very name.

None of them ever refer to a precise ideological and historical tradition, but rather point to some generic attitude or value ("disobedience," "standing," "alive," "moving," "we can," "momentum," etc.), vague enough not to foreclose any new support. Just as the mass party remained the default form of politics in the Fordist era, the "digital party," "party movement," or "platform party" always worked as the political twin of the start-up company. This faster politics—a sort of collage using the leftovers of the traditional political families as its raw material—has proven extremely efficient in at least one case: in a context marked by the simultaneous collapse of the center-left and center-right, and with the help of benevolent media coverage, Macron's hollow shell (LREM) proved the ideal vehicle for driving the candidate to two consecutive electoral successes.

Even when it did not lead to outright victories, as in Macron's scenario, this new "business model" has reversed a three-decade-long trend: the hemorrhaging participation rate in traditional parties. At their peak, the left-populist start-ups could boast respectable membership numbers: in 2017, Podemos and LFI claimed between 500,000 and 550,000 registered members, which, while lagging way behind the good ol' mass parties of yesterday, nonetheless placed them far ahead of national competitors. Even in a much more traditional party such as Labour, membership rates ballooned under Corbyn—doubling between 2014 and 2015, reaching a peak of 564,000 registered fee-paying members in December 2017 (which made it the largest party in Western Europe at the time) before reverting to a slow but steady decline.[6] While golden-age membership numbers were still out of reach—in 1952–53, Labour hit no less than a million members—the figures marked a clear break from New Labour complacency. One conclusion seemed undeniable.

Left populists had successfully mobilized a massive reserve army to campaign for them during election season. They did so by radically lowering the barriers to entry, multiplying incentives for cheap affiliation, and blurring the line between members and non-members.

This produced some tangible results. When positioned as outsiders, their organizational experiments and the rebirth of militancy they fostered were premised on a sharp critique of traditional political parties, which they cast as antidemocratic, ossified, and subject to bureaucratic capture. They targeted the contemporary "iron law of oligarchy," according to which political parties tend to develop an internal aristocracy made up of highly active militants, insiders who stand in the way of newcomers and whose *raison d'être* is their own self-preservation, thus leading to a certain bureaucratic stasis—a defect which Podemos figurehead Pablo Iglesias typified as the left's "senile disorder." Against these tendencies, the new political challengers, including left populists, have come to harbor strong antiparty sentiments and to produce a narrative articulated around the democratic benefits of online collective deliberation.[7] The web, they announced, had finally provided the technical means to organize collective action and discussion between equals on a mass scale. It was the democratic tool par excellence, dooming the intermediary layers of the parties' bureaucracy to natural obsolescence. To varying extents, all left-populist contenders have espoused such an antimediation narrative—even if some of them have, like Podemos, proposed a hybrid model rather than a complete rejection of the classical form of party organization. In that regard, they were all children of their era.

The participatory limits of this model swiftly revealed them-selves. The coalition of actors involved in the local groups was often particularly diverse and fragile. Left populism's catch-all approach brought together people who would not willingly participate in the same political organization over the long haul. As one local militant told us in an interview, her "action group" in La France insoumise was a disorderly affair—where authentic leftist militants were campaigning alongside right-wing conspiracy theorists—only held together by the prospect of Mélenchon's election. In addition, most of the newcomers maintained a relatively low level of involve-ment, thus rendering the rebound in membership and participa-tion fragile in all the cases under scrutiny. Just one year after Keir Starmer climbed to the top of the mast at Labour, party membership had dropped by a fifth.[8] Two years after the 2017 French presidential election, La France insoumise's rank and file had been decimated, as the movement counted 60,000 members. It was as easy to get out as it had been to get in. The same sixty-six-year-old communist activist who praised Mélenchon's oratory skills bitterly regretted that, when he started to have doubts about LFI's line, all he had to do was to "unsubscribe" from the mailing list. Afterward, no one ever inquired into his reasons for leaving. Moreover, in the absence of a verifiable list of fee-paying members, the figures claimed by these parties were often misleading. It has been estimated, for instance, that La France insoumise's "action groups" were significantly smaller than declared and that only 25 percent of them were genuinely active, which would divide the official census by ten (from 60,000 to 6,000).[9] In Podemos, less than half the sympathizers were deemed to be active. Finally, the introduction, in 2020, of a three-euro fee to be registered to the local circles revealed the true number of properly militant *podemitas*: around 19,000.[10]

This problem was only compounded by the diffuse command structure of many left-populist outfits. Although they claimed to have abolished the distinction between core militants and mere sympathizers—no privileges were granted to the former—hierarchies soon asserted themselves. In fact, research has repeatedly proved that the gap between members and voters persists: the former are still more likely to be men, with a higher level of education and a better employment status than the latter. Among members too, de facto hierarchies returned, as the different levels of activism progressively divided the core militants from more sporadic participants. Functioning as a *swarm*,[11] where atomized individuals play their part in a common strategy decreed by an unmentioned queen bee, this kind of political formation must rely on the work of "super-volunteers" to compensate for the lack of permanent staff.[12] As Bernie's advisors had it in their blueprint, "The revolution will not be staffed." Such informality often implies a real risk of exacerbating rather than decreasing inequalities among activists; that is, between those who can afford full-time voluntary activism and those who cannot. The annals of LFI are full of testimonies along these lines. Charlotte Girard, a central figure of the 2017 campaign and wife of Mélenchon's late right-hand man, François Delapierre, openly criticized the lack of adjustment for a full-time working single mother eager to play an important role in the organization. Others lamented the "Parisianism" of the movement. LFI's "super-volunteers" thus became a sort of new internal oligarchy, far more active than the large mass of apathetic, "lurking" supporters, sporadically active in online consultations at best. The research is indisputable: the dream of online collective deliberation never materialized. Rather, it rapidly turned into a new plebiscitary model. Most of the online consultations amounted to a form of "pseudo-participation"[13] that "almost invariably ended with supermajority splits in favor of the line chosen by the leadership."[14]

All in all, these attacks on the very idea of mediation aggravated the issues of representation which left populists first set out to solve. It implied overinvestment in the "war of movement," the use of organizational and communicational shortcuts to conquer executive power as if *by surprise*. This was to be achieved through electoral blitz and digital agitprop, which failed to address the terrifying complexity of the issues facing socialist governments. By insisting on a strict equation between power and electoral returns, left populists were bound to end up prioritizing form over content and quantity over quality. The return to politics they pushed for, understood as a performance of antagonism, tended to hollow out the policy content they endorsed. It set aside the crucial issues for later: how to escape from the EU's fiscal bite? How to reconcile working-class and middle-class views on environmental issues? How to deal with claims for regional autonomy? Many left populists were short of any clear answers to these questions. For classical socialism, the commitment to internationalism at least offered a generic way of dealing with national issues.

Lacking this asset, left populism was destined to run into the same obstacles over and over again: to indulge in the same fascination as neoliberals for technocratic fixes, and to accentuate the current disjunction between the realms of politics and policy. Indeed, some scholars have argued that populism and technocracy share a natural complicity.

This haphazard collage is hardly a replacement for solid party structures. While avoiding the traps of bureaucratic immobilism is certainly commendable, the aversion toward sturdier political organization might soon backfire. Left populists have, so far, failed to build long-lasting loyalties among their militants and voters. Instead, they have mostly settled for passive and superficial bonds with their constituency, which accommodate rather than subvert the neoliberal order. This start-up approach also carries risk. Except for (rare) moments of profound dislocation (such as the one that occurred in the wake of the subprime crisis), it could simply fall flat. The parallel fates of the movements hubristically set up by Matteo Renzi (Italia Viva) and Íñigo Errejón (Más País), condemned to marginality after they left their respective parties (Democratic Party and Podemos), are telling in this regard—it was exceedingly difficult to summon a political force out of the blue with little but a well-oiled PR machine. Through its excessive reliance on electoral payoffs and digital engagement, they run the risk of becoming the victims of the same volatility that brought them into the spotlight in the first place. Without laying foundations in society, they might turn out to be little more than a flash in the pan, extinguished by the next blast of wind—a scenario that almost became reality for the Italian Five Star

Movement. Without entrenching the party into coherent voting blocs, without recreating social bonds and a specific subculture, without providing the popular sectors with a crucible in which to build a collective view of society, and without training a new generation of cadres beyond the star player—in sum, without waging a war of position to consolidate the gains of the digital vanguard—left populism will be remembered as little more than a wasted opportunity.

Where did all the populists go? That was the question posed by journalists at the *Guardian* in early 2021, surveying the state of left politics at the peak of the COVID crisis. Over the previous five years, the left had been remarkably open about its populist commitments. Now, references to the populist label were becoming increasingly scarce, and readings of Laclau's *On Populist Reason* a rarity. The populist moment had ground to a halt. Feeding off the relative disarray of social democratic parties and the increasing disorganization of party democracy after the credit crash, left populists had tried to cohere a new cross-class coalition. In 2021, as COVID put classical Western politics on hold, a balance sheet could finally be compiled. What did it achieve and where did it fail? Yet "Who Has Changed and Who Is Dead?" was a more appropriate question. As the players deserted the pitch, odds for the next season were already being calculated: Mélenchon readied himself for the next election, Bernie went back to senatorial brokering, Podemos shuffled together a governing coalition, and Corbyn decided to simply reclaim a seat in the Commons.

How these figures would regroup in the new decade was an

open question. In total, five possible scenarios seemed on offer, with the populist left either remaining or exiting from the scene entirely. As the 2010s gave way to the 2020s, the underlying structural factors which lent the populist hypothesis its original plausibility had hardly shifted, from decaying party structures to ongoing credit crises. In all cases, however, it proved difficult to turn the explosion into a bombing campaign.

Paradoxically, one of left populism's main problems has also been the partial death of the world described by Mair. Rather than a complete void, there has only been a relative erosion of the classical party system: people continue to vote on the basis of class, and parties and trade unions have not disappeared all at once. In some countries they have stubbornly resisted decline and continue to play an important role in political life—think of the Spanish socialists or the Belgian trade-union movements. Even in cases where the decline of mainstream actors has been spectacular (the Greek and French socialists) not all their organs have disappeared simultaneously; in the end, for left populists, the "void" was never quite empty enough.

An incomplete void has also meant that left populists' achievements tended to be more rhetorical than real. Once populists had had their go at winning a majority—think of Podemos's failed *sorpasso* of the Spanish socialists, or Jean-Luc Mélenchon's return to a classical left-wing platform—they usually sought to make peace with mainstream parties. This entailed positioning themselves on a left–right axis, or forging alliances with traditional politicians. Most painfully, however, left populists have had to "institutionalize," shelving slogans like "beyond left and right" and giving up on their claim to represent "the 99 percent," restricting themselves to a narrower social base. Yet once "the populist moment" had passed, left populists tended to face internal party divisions and unbreakable electoral ceilings. Despite frantic predictions of imminent collapse, the center did, in fact, hold, and several center-left parties reclaimed their place in governing coalitions, from Germany to Spain. The left came up with a variety of survival tactics in this new environment, either retreating into the domesticity of established far-left spaces or embracing increasingly brazen types of PR politics. Together they offer a biography of the left *after* its populist phase.

5.

FIVE SCENARIOS

At the end of Jorge Semprún's novel *La Algarabía* (1981), the author contemplates a provocative counterfactual. What if the 1968 student revolt had succeeded where the Parisian Commune had failed, and Paris remained a red city? Rather than being dispersed by de Gaulle, the students and workers seize the reins of power in the French capital—but fail to make it into the provinces. The red flag flies on the Seine, but remains isolated. At the end of the 1970s, the small communist city state is still holding out and becomes a free port for refugees. Rather than a global uprising, the revolution is confined to one single municipality and lives with a siege mentality, a libertine oasis shielded from the rest of the world.

As the last remnants of the 2011 protest wave died down and the camps on Syntagma were cleared away, the scenario set out by Semprún resonated with many left populists. What exactly remained of the populist left after the post-2008 cycle? And how could one appraise its performance over that time span? Like Semprún's radicals, some had retreated into the cities. At its onset, Podemos promised to occupy the space left vacant by Spanish social democracy. Politics, like nature, abhors a vacuum. Retrospectively, the populist left's role across the 2010s seems, indeed, to have consisted in revitalizing the left, after its main social democrat representatives had surrendered to the siren calls of neoliberalism. *Contra* those who cried wolf about populism's alleged "radicalism," it was never designed as a revolutionary form of politics. Rather, it was an attempt at updating the reformist project by other means. In fact, Podemos claimed to be a moderate reaction against the real radicalism—the brutal transformation of societies operated by neoliberals—and many observers have rightly pointed out that *l'avenir en commun* was, in many respects, less radical a political program than Mitterrand's when he was first elected president in 1981. Neither would Tsipras, Corbyn, or Sanders style themselves revolutionaries: the fact that they appeared so radical to many observers merely showed how far the ideological center of gravity had veered to the right. The left's populist turn did not result from a sudden radical surge; it was made possible by the opening of a representative void which it sought to fill. This void was the outcome of a twofold process: the long-term erosion of political representation in Western democracies, and the management of the subprime crisis by political elites, including the established center-left.

The emphasis here remains on a populist left rather than a left populism. The fate of today's populism—much like that of its historical precedents in the United States and Russia at the end of the nineteenth century and in Latin America throughout the twentieth—is intimately tied to the fading fortunes of social democracy in the current century. Where the preconditions are not met for the development of social democracy—either because the groups it purports to represent have yet to be organized, as in the examples cited above, or because they are in a state of advanced decomposition, as today—populism will become the default mode of politics. Populism, in other words, is a form of *social democracy without social democracy*, or the form taken by progressive politics in times of (relative) disorganization.

In this vein, many observers have retrospectively interpreted the American populist episode of the late nineteenth century as the functional equivalent of European social democracy; in fact, many US policy reforms introduced from the early 1910s to the New Deal were directly borrowed from a populist playbook. Contrary to its predecessors, however, contemporary populism has thrived in a context of declining, rather than rising, mass politics, which has shaped its current dynamics and set hard limits on its transformative potential.

Beyond the relatively similar setbacks endured by left-populist contenders, these forces have followed various trajectories resulting from the interplay between a specific context (electoral rules, party system, socio-economic situation, structure of political cleavages, etc.) and a peculiar interpretation of the populist hypothesis. Most importantly, whether as insiders or outsiders—whether trying to take over an existing party machine or building a new vehicle from scratch—the journey of populists is always tied to that of an established center-left party. Did the old party machine merely sputter, as in the US, or did it fall into the clutches of the contender, as in the UK? Did the infamous process of "Pasokification" happen, in whole or just in part? In Syriza's experience, when the social democratic competitor collapsed entirely, it paved the way for populism to conquer power on its own, thereby prematurely testing its capacity to resist institutionalization and achieve real policy successes. In a case of near-Pasokification, like the French Socialist Party, the populist formation was empowered to become the hegemonic force on the left and to reorganize this political space along its own lines. Where the old social democratic party resisted, as the Spanish PSOE did, it forced the left-populist challenger into cohabitation, allowing it to reach executive power from a minority position. Faced with these constraints, each strategic choice led to divergent outcomes, and left distinct policy legacies. Surveying these journeys, it is possible to delineate five distinct scenarios, or futures. They provide a tentative list of the possible gains of the left-populist gamble.

Disappearance: Corbynism

There were worse options, of course. After Jeremy Corbyn stepped down as Labour leader in January 2020, a contest ensued between Rebecca Long-Bailey and Keir Starmer. Formerly shadow Brexit secretary, the latter had proven instrumental in steering the party away from its Northern Leave-voting base and maintaining ties with the old guard. Yet he also proved abidingly popular with the remaining membership base. Demoralized and disorganized, the original Corbynite faction either defected to Starmer or tried to rally behind Long-Bailey. The continuity between the Corbyn bloc and the Starmer coalition also proved uncomfortable. Many of the fiscal orthodoxies of the 2010s now proved an electoral liability. Cheap credit and low interest rates had kept together a coalition of affluent homeowners and City capital, again cornering the metropolitan working class which Corbynism had tried to rally. Even if the rise of inflation brought out cracks in this coalition, the weakness of any oppositional force assured continued Tory rule. Corbynism's response to the first dilemma was to weld together a class of falling metropolitan voters with the older Labour voters in the North. More than the dilemma posed in trying to appeal to middle and working classes, which Labour faced in the twentieth century, this question was compounded by the disorganization of Labour's civil society since the 1980s. Building a digital party through Momentum, or simulating that older civil society, proved no real substitute for a vanished substructure. Instead, the members either left en masse or were actively pushed out, returning Labour to its old cartel form. Now, the route was open for the Starmerites to re-establish ties with the Blair generation and seek allies in the Treasury and the Bank of England, whose views on fiscal matters were edging closer to their own.

This was, in many ways, a bleak outcome for the populist left in Britain. Unlike their French or Spanish comrades, they had no room for a party challenger. Yet they did have the advantage of being able to use an established party machine for their own ends, which greatly reduced the costs encountered by Podemos and La France insoumise. The risk of wounded attachment to a party inimical to its desires thereby also increased: rather than an instrument to be deployed at will, the Labour Party warped Corbynism's priorities. It turned out the party was using them, and not the other way around. This interiority made marginalization all but inevitable: they had to amputate themselves to signal disaffiliation with the outfit, or tie themselves to a corpse.

After the decline of Corbynism, challenges to the left of the party could once more be contemplated. The Enough Is Enough campaign did try to remedy this decoupling by firmly basing itself in the existing union movement. On the whole, however, the pull of Labour remained persistently strong even for Corbynite survivors. Both inside and outside the party, the loyalty remained overwhelming. As such, this was the worst option for the left populists: their policy kit had been plundered by outsiders, while their intrinsic ties to the party made it difficult to initiate a messy break. No government participation and few policy legacies spelled the liquidation of Corbynism. This was reflected on the level of personnel, too: virtually none of the cadre remained in the party, deserting for other outfits. At the close of 2021, Corbyn himself was ejected from the party by Starmer, only escaping deselection by retaining an independent seat in the House of Commons. The ultimate intention of the "Starmer project"—to erase not just references to but also memories of the Corbynite moment—was crystal clear.[1]

Credit, the lifeline on which British politics has relied for a generation, would be in increasingly low supply. During the few weeks in which Truss was in power, there was much talk of the libertarian takeover of the Tories led by Britain's pro-market think tanks. Yet as hired agents they were also secondary to the old nexus between the Treasury, Bank of England, and the City of London, which the Truss government has now inadvertently tied back together in opposition to her short-lived plans. The resurgent trade-union movement has thus far proved to be the only faction in society willing to increase labor's share of income. That this militancy has risen during a period in which the Labour Party's leadership has been at times actively hostile to worker organization began to weaken ideas that the party could prove a catalyst for mass mobilization. Impressively, over 87,000 days were lost as a result of strike action in July 2022 alone; the yearly average for 2019 was 19,500. Corbynism felt like a distant memory for the movement.

This liquidation also expressed itself on the international stage. In May 2022, affiliates of La France insoumise organized a rally which Corbyn attended, as a fellow left-populist sympathizer. The media backlash proved ferocious, with Parisian journalists castigating Mélenchon and his party for allying with an "antisemite." The association was too risky by now, and showed the fissuring of the transnational links the populist left had built up in the preceding five years. With the disaggregation of individual components, the left's informal international of populists also began to fray. The weakest link again proved the Corbynite connection, which had not only lost control of its party but seemed tainted even to foreign affiliates. Corbyn did not so much retreat as vanish, unable to even wage a campaign for the London mayoralty. "They made a desert and called it peace."

Normalization: Podemos

If Corbyn presented the worst case—out of power, out of politics—the Spanish experiment appeared relatively enviable. Observed from a strictly technical perspective, Podemos's journey since its inception looks like a success story. Usually, newcomers in a party system fail to stabilize their presence in the long run (for political scientists, inertia is the rule, disruption the exception). Unlike the many single-issue parties that emerged to fragment Western party systems over the past decades, however, Podemos's project was set at a much higher benchmark. Like its Greek and French left-populist cousins, it had the explicit objective of conquering power and displacing social democracy altogether. Podemos deliberately put into practice the populist instruction manual with the aim of building a new majority in Spain. The plan was then to establish alliances at the European level, and ultimately to redraw the architecture of the eurozone. For this reason, many *podemitas* saw failure where others saw resounding success. This created a discrepancy between two possible readings: neither conquest nor defeat.

This midway position was not of Podemos's own choosing. The rise of new contenders at the national level—Ciudadanos, followed by Vox—had a double effect: it ate away at Podemos's novelty as a party and re-established the left–right axis for political competition. Even more decisive, however, was the reorientation of the PSOE after the party's stormy leadership election. Despite the revolt of local barons, led by Susana Díaz, which provoked the temporary resignation of Pedro Sánchez, the latter eventually managed to turn the tide: rejuvenating the party's image, endorsing a left turn by distancing himself firmly from the conservatives and borrowing some of Podemos's ideas, and showing (at least on the surface) openness toward alliance on its left while aiming for a government of its own, supported from outside. The latter scenario finally played out in 2018—appointed prime minister in June, Sánchez agreed on a budget with Podemos in October.

The PSOE's reputation now seemed fully restored: it was back as a pivotal force on the center-left and as the most trustworthy alternative to the right. The socialists' strategic shift, initiated as early as 2016, put Podemos in a double bind. The dispute between Iglesias and Errejón, largely a quarrel over what attitude to adopt vis-à-vis the socialists, was not only the reflection of two different interpretations of the populist creed—agonism vs. transversality. It was also a sign of Iglesias's much weaker faith in the blueprint they had drawn up in the middle of the 2010s: to him, populism was nothing more than a disposable tool for lifting the authentic left away from the margins and up toward heaven. As a result, Iglesias's victory over his erstwhile lieutenant sanctioned the exhaustion of Podemos's populist moment and the start of a long process of normalization.

This metamorphosis was clear for all to see: from a scrappy

challenger on the left, Podemos progressively became a party much like any other. First, the party underwent a strong institutionalization process—its parliamentary group absorbing an increasing amount of its resources as the party structure itself stiffened under Iglesias's leadership—that alienated the social movements whose political translation it was once supposed to be. Second, Podemos repudiated its initial novelty vis-à-vis the whole Spanish political system—"the regime of 1978"—to embrace a much more accommodating discourse. This was articulated around the necessity to return to the Constitution of 1978 which the governing parties had betrayed. In parallel, it reduced its ambitions, for it had ceased to be credible as the new majority force of the country. Third, its electoral performances stabilized within a much more modest range, between 10 and 15 percent of the vote, well below its first aspirations and more in line with the "normal" weight of a radical left force. Finally, the party explicitly and comfortably repositioned itself along the left–right axis through its alliance with the far-left Izquierda Unida. This was coupled with a clear return to an antifascist discourse targeting Vox and the PP's most reactionary fringes, a growing "special relationship" with the PSOE, and a rehabilitation of the leftist symbols it had carefully sidelined during its populist moment.

Now, at the end of this cycle, Podemos does not look much like the broad national-popular umbrella of which Errejón and his inner circle had dreamt. Despite the disintegration of Spanish politics in the 2010s, Europe was never going to become South America—"Latin Americanization" was a tendency, not a fate. The established parties proved more resilient than many observers had expected, particularly in the case of the PSOE when, during the 2015–16 electoral marathon, Podemos seemed to have a real chance of winning the race for the executive. The old parties' entrenchment within the state, their frail yet privileged bonds with civil society, their monopoly in the rural areas, and their greater capacity for renewal—drawn from a considerable pool of human resources—enabled them to bend without ever breaking. The left–right axis persisted. Contrary to appearances, Spanish social democracy did not vacate its space and showed remarkable resilience in the medium term. The rise of a challenger forced it to draw on its innermost resources to maintain its position at the top of left politics in Spain. The results were ironic, certainly when seen from afar. Rather than killing off the Socialist Party and taking its place, Podemos indirectly lifted the ailing ruler back onto his throne. Podemos's historical function has in fact consisted in reviving and rejuvenating social democracy. The presence of a contender on their left flank forced the socialists to renew their political style and ideological commitments. At the end of the day, Podemos acted as a gatekeeper preventing the socialists from turning their back on their left-wing electorate. It thereby avoided an Italian-style scenario (the complete implosion of the centre-left), and prevented the neo-Francoist right from standing as the only radical alternative to established parties. Along the way, it was able to add several progressive policy points on the national agenda, on both the socio-economic and cultural front. Podemos thus lays claim to a real legacy of success, even though its margin for growth is now drastically curtailed and a role as the PSOE's auxiliary seems to be its only real prospect.

Reordering: La France insoumise

The message was clear: here was a bunch of "leftists," "radicals," "extremists," a hotbed of "Islamo-leftists," plotting against the Republic. In the wake of the 2022 legislative elections, these were epithets used all over the French media to disqualify LFI and the coalition it had managed to bring together, the Nouvelle union populaire écologique et sociale. A strange consensus was taking shape against Mélenchon's troops: they were now anathema to both nationalist and centrist blocs, respectively dominated by Marine Le Pen and Emmanuel Macron. Only a month earlier Macron was flirting with the left and appealing to its "responsibility" against the brown menace. Now, the two finalists of the presidential election were vilifying the third bloc, to whom the polls were giving a tiny but real chance of getting a majority in parliament. The *péril rouge* narrative—forty years earlier, Michel Poniatowski, Valéry Giscard d'Estaing's interior minister, predicted that Soviet tanks would invade Paris in the event of a Mitterrand victory—was dusted off for the occasion. The far right's supposedly antisystemic nature was also revealed at this time for what it always was: a convenient disguise for opportunism. Overall, it was telling to discover how far the public debate had moved to the right. The most important lesson, however, went unnoticed by most commentators: it exposed the limits, in the long run, of LFI's strategy and the ceiling into which it repeatedly hit. How come a party that was accused—only a couple of years earlier—of playing into the hands of the far right with its protectionist stances, had suddenly become a den of bloodthirsty anarchists and Bolsheviks?

The moment quickly sent commentators back to the well-springs of the LFI experiment. Their crusade's origins went back to 2005, when the referendum on the EU constitution created a split between two factions of the left: the pro-European and liberal-adjacent one, dominated by the socialists, and the antiliberal and Euroskeptic one. *La gauche de la gauche*, "the left of the left," authentically social and ecological, was on the rise. The vote against the EU acted as the founding moment that gave this bloc its ideological coherence and established its autonomy from the other, more market-friendly left. It was one of the decisive steps in the disintegration of the two blocs, left and right, that had contended for power since the onset of the Fifth Republic. Together with two other triggers—the rise of the far right and Macron's unification of center-right and center-left forces—this created a new field of competition. It was organized around three rival blocs, none of which could achieve hegemony. Until recently, however, the third bloc remained highly fragmented. It was also still lagging behind the socialists, who had not yet undergone full implosion and had been capable of winning a presidential contest as recently as 2012. Mélenchon's oscillations since he left the Socialist Party in 2008 tell the adventurous story of how this third bloc united and delivered the *coup de grâce* to the party refounded by Mitterrand at Épinay in 1971.

In this story, LFI's populist and digital turn in 2016 played a paradoxical role. Mélenchon and his disciples were never sincere *errejonistas*. Unlike the founding circle of Podemos, their faith in populism was instrumental and circumstantial. Notwithstanding their admiration for Venezuela's Bolivarian leaders and the Citizens' Revolution in Ecuador, they never believed that a national-popular regime was the most likely or even desirable option for France. Their understanding of populism was doubtless closer to Iglesias's: it was a tool that could help the authentic left become, against all odds, the established force in French society at large. Therein lay the paradox: Mélenchon and his troops did not achieve their stated objective, but instead the one they had openly repudiated. While they failed to make the authentic left hegemonic, they succeeded in gaining hegemonic sway over it. Populism's digital savvy proved decisive in this regard. In a context marked by the disqualification of the signifier "left" itself, the crumbling of old political blocs, and the atomization of society, it offered the best-adapted vehicle to navigate the void, as was proved in the 2017 presidential contest. After the election and five years of constant polemics between the factions of the third bloc (*insoumis*, communists, Trotskyists, left greens, and socialist dissidents), Mélenchon's rising star left little room for doubt: LFI was at the helm. Within two weeks, all the other factions would rally around it. This was not sufficient, however, to achieve a majority, let alone political hegemony. The wild red-baiting and media-generated panic were the most conspicuous sign of this failure: the third bloc, despite its impressive numbers on election day, could still be written off as marginal and radical. Repeated bouts of reported friction between the coalition partners, meanwhile, signaled the fragility of LFI's internal leadership.

The episode demonstrated both the strengths and weaknesses of LFI. As clever as it was, its response to both dilemmas—how to bring together the heterogeneous low and middle classes, how to move swiftly through the fragmented landscape of the 2010s—was at best incomplete. The terms of debate had changed considerably since the 1970s, when communists and socialists were smiling to each other's faces while sharpening the knives behind their backs. Roughly speaking, back then, the communists were betting on the working class, while the socialists were championing the civil and public servant class (in fact, the socialist party was often labeled "the party of teachers"). The demographic equation for the 2010s, however, was far more complex. The potential support for a left bloc was split between the declining working class of post-industrial areas, the rural and semi-rural population of *la France périphérique*, and the three categories hit hardest by the 2008 crisis: the urban educated youth ("connected outsiders"), the squeezed middle class, and the new precariat of the urban and suburban regions.

The populist approach enabled LFI to bind the last three together and thus to secure its leadership position within the left. It proved less adept, however, at reaching its other two objectives, themselves necessary conditions to build a hegemonic bloc: bringing the working class back into the fold and penetrating the rural constituencies. Those two categories were still tempted by the abstentionist or the far-right options. The vote for Mélenchon remained an essentially urban and suburban one. On the other hand, LFI's adoption of a light and agile structure proved crucial to mobilization in a context where individuals were atomized and disaffiliated. However, it rendered the new bloc less solid than in the past, as there was no structure capable of facilitating its entrenchment into society in the long run. LFI's hegemony on the left is a relatively frail one.

Mélenchon's journey over the past decade thus outlines a possible scenario for the populist left. The populist turn can indeed bring about the profound renewal and reordering of the left across the board. It may even precipitate the death of a social democratic dinosaur, without necessarily offering the sweetness of electoral victory. To be fair, we would probably be assessing this entire venture very differently had Mélenchon secured only 420,000 more votes in the latest presidential election. There are ample reasons to believe, however, that a Mélenchon presidency would not have radically altered the rules of game: without a horizon capable of holding together the heterogeneous coalition of social groups, and without an organizational model capable of growing strong roots into those same groups, it is likely that the third bloc in government would have been both fragile internally and disappointing in terms of policy outcomes. Majoritarian, but not hegemonic. Or as the patient advocates of Syriza would put it, in office but not in power.

Neutralization: Syriza

On April 14, 2022, Alexis Tsipras addressed a calm and well-behaved crowd at his party's convention. Before he began, two foreign leaders appeared successively on the giant screen to give a short speech: Yolanda Díaz, Pablo Iglesias's successor in the Spanish government, and António Costa, the socialist prime minister of Portugal. Both insisted on the necessity of building bridges between progressive forces. The populist left should team up with social democrats. Tsipras could not agree more, and he called on other Greek progressives to unite under the leadership of Syriza with a view to the next elections. The European alliance of socialists had, for a while, been looking upon Tsipras with positive benevolence. A few months before Syriza's convention, a member of the PES anonymously admitted what anyone could plainly feel: "PASOK is our member but, ideologically speaking, we are on the same page as Mr. Tsipras." Ironically, this flirtation revealed that Pasokification, at the end of the day, could be read both ways: as the virtual disappearance of a social democratic party, or as the "social-democratization" of the populist left.

This rapprochement was the logical outcome of Syriza's evolution. It presents a scenario in which the populist left is completely emptied of its subversive potential while retaining its single other ambition: to conquer power and keep it. And yet Syriza had provided an adequate response to the dilemmas of the left. Its modern style of communication had proved capable of reaching out to voters far beyond the circles of the organized left. It had built unity out of heterogeneity by finding the common ground between the middle and lower classes: their resolute opposition to austerity. At the same time, over the protests of its own left faction, it had reached most voters by navigating an ambiguous and moderate path out of the crisis: opposing the memoranda while banishing the idea of Grexit.

This proved to be an extremely taxing balancing act. The middle ground that Tsipras and his inner circle pursued on the economic issues was certainly the precondition required to convince a majority of voters. But it also made it impossible to deliver on Syriza's promises to them. At least one of two conditions needed to be fulfilled for this position to succeed: either a robust international alliance disposed to put pressure on the creditors, or a relatively accommodating attitude from the latter at the table. Tsipras miscalculated the likelihood of both—with François Hollande ruling France as any moderate liberal would and Wolfgang Schaüble holding the purse strings during negotiations, both paths were foreclosed.

These obstacles were, to a large extent, the product of the particular position in which Greece found itself, at the very heart of the eurozone's asymmetries. The populist approach, however, was not blameless: in fact, it consisted in circum-venting the problem rather than facing it. The productive ambiguity—no memorandum, no Grexit—necessary to build a large coalition and keep everyone happy could lead only to resounding failure during negotiations. This points to a limit that seems inherent to populism: lacking both the thorough economic analysis and the strong international imagination that have characterized the labor movement throughout history, the populist approach always risks ending up in lukewarm economic policies and narrow nationalism.

The Greek disaster did not end there, however. Syriza's capitulation drove an entire country into political, not just the international left. Tsipras's narrow victory in the elections he called in September 2015 was obtained by default, in the absence of a real alternative—since January of the same year, the voter turnout had fallen by 7.5 percentage points. Now he was back in charge but, having already renounced his pledge and made the protesters desert the streets, what was next? As Stathis Kouvelakis observed, just as happened to Achille Occhetto, the former head of the PCI who went into ecstasies over the temples of capitalism he found in Manhattan, the collapse of Tsipras's inner world led to a total nihilism. Besides becoming the most zealous servant of Greece's creditors, Tsipras openly aligned his foreign policy with Atlantic interests—which notably meant going back on his word to break away from pro-Israeli policies. The U-turn was complete.

All this sheds light on the infantile symptoms of populist politics: in the event of policy failure, the (relative) lack of ideological consistency and the heterogeneous constituency yield no good options for tactical retreats. It thus switches straight to the default mode of politics: opportunism and clientelism. The electoral machine becomes a den of wolves concerned only to maintain their position. Syriza's relative resilience in the 2019 general election—although it lost, it did not collapse—cannot be explained by the ideological loyalty of specific sociological sectors. The map of its results tells another story: it performed well in the former strongholds of PASOK, whose client base it inherited. This is not the least of populism's paradoxes: born with a strong antipolitical impulse, it can easily turn into its opposite and become a mere vehicle for power-hungry opportunists. Just as Syriza's ranks are stuffed with arrivistes who dream of becoming the new Papandreou, the Five Star Movement is now host to many potential new Andreottis. The title of Luigi Di Maio's 2021 book sums it up perfectly: *Un amore chiamato politica* (A Love Story Called Politics). A neat way to distance himself from the "antipolitical" reputation of the movement he once led.

Splintering: Sanders

Were there any midway options between uneasy normalization and total collapse? Unlike the UK, the United States does not have a Labour Party, in which trade unions and workers are integrated into party power. Precisely because Bernie has never been able to rely on a party machinery, he has built up an organization of his own. He might run on Democratic platforms and take part in their primaries, but his organizational resources do not depend on big money donors and DNC personnel. It was long said that Bernie would suffer from the absence of a sustainable party superstructure in the United States. Corbyn, in turn, managed to infiltrate an already existing party and colonize it for his own purposes. But this colonization was never complete, and the rebel elements were never expelled. Corbynism never managed to control its boisterous, Europhile middle classes, inconstant in their loyalties and flaky in their politics. These fair-weather friends remained far more existentially wedded to EU membership than they were to socialism—even when it was made clear that Europe would be a major obstacle to key points of the Labour manifesto like railway nationalization, even when the barbarous cruelty of the EU to migrants was exposed, and even when the financial benefits of economic integration remained so low.

From March 2020 onward, both the exigencies of the COVID crisis and mounting GOP authoritarianism found the American constitutional order beginning to crack at the seams. For Bernie, this posed a real dilemma. The brazenly antidemocratic maneuvers of the GOP forced him to rely on the Democratic Party. The passing of the Trump and Biden checks could be attributed to Democratic pressure, even if the "business community" remained overwhelmingly in favor of the measures. The Green New Deal proved abortive, while the final climate bill flopped. What, then, was the balance sheet of his millennial socialism? Did they shift the conversation, or did they simply hasten a previous process of class dealignment?

These were real policy legacies. Yet they came with a painful catch: loyalty to the DNC bloc and electoral bargaining inside the parameters of the old regime. Bernie protested against Joe Manchin's recalcitrance; AOC did insist that in any properly functioning party democracy, Manchin and she would not find themselves in the same party. Yet this wish did not change the calculus in which she was caught. Congressional discipline would reassert itself. The Bernie bloc had consolidated itself precisely due to the weakness of the Democrats as a party, which has revealed itself to be more of a state department than anything else. But this also implied working as a surrogate within the party itself. It allowed Bernites to maintain a critical distance which the Corbynites lacked. But it also put them in a position too close for comfort for a frontal assault. Without being held hostage, they were on friendlier terms with the Democrats now, but by the same token were forced to collaborate even more openly. The combo of dealignment and calcification—in which a growing group of floating voters was simultaneously flanked by two hardening cores on either side—kneecapped the "class-struggle social democracy" proposed by the Bernie coalition.[2] This was not liquidation, of course—but it was anything but a victory. Not only were the Bernites easily snuffed out by the internal machinations of the Democratic leadership, but all the energy, data, and infrastructure of the campaign went up in smoke around April 2020, leaving little trace behind. The demobilizing effect of the pandemic certainly played a role; as Benjamin Fong noted, "senior staff members added a line to their CVs and moved on."

Most election campaigns end with a whimper, not a bang. But Bernie also set a different benchmark. In 2016, there was at least one attempt to translate the campaign into a lasting organization—Our Revolution. For a variety of reasons, including the simple fact that the Democratic Socialists of America (DSA) stole its thunder, Our Revolution didn't pan out, but the basic impulse was a good one: to use the election cycle to generate data, activists, and strategies that could be transferred into a more permanent organization. Indeed, for those who always thought that Democrats would never let Bernie win, this was the chief reason to support Bernie's candidacies. The first conceptual hurdle to overcome Bernie and the Squad's relative disinterest in institution-building, which might be reason enough to relegate the idea to the realm of fantasy. Nevertheless, a third primary race for the presidency could change the calculus. If the campaign was conceived from the outset as being not about 2024 but about what 2024 will leave behind, many would see it differently: it would be about committing to the establishment of a sustainable left-wing counterweight to the duopoly, rather than just another quixotic attempt from within a party of capital. The question remains.

Conclusion
POPULISM'S NEXT DECADE

Halfway through her "collective autobiography" *The Years*, French writer Annie Ernaux offers her readers a political panorama of the early 1990s:

> The rumor was going round that politics was dead. The advent of a "new world order" was declared. The End of History was nigh . . . The word "struggle" was discredited as a throwback to Marxism, became an object of ridicule. As for "defending rights," the first that came to mind were those of the consumer.[1]

Born to working-class parents in 1940, Ernaux had already grown to be one of her country's most celebrated writers by the end of the 2000s. Published in French in 2008, her "collective autobiography" about post-war French society appeared shortly before Lehman Brothers went bust. An English translation came out only in 2017, already at the close of the populist decade.

When it was first published, Ernaux's memoir diagnosed a shuttered and claustral world in which people had retreated into privacy, where politics was relegated to the back burner while technocrats were in charge. Tony Blair claimed that opposing globalization was like opposing the changing of the seasons, while the term "*Alternativlosigkeit*" (lack of an alternative) entered the German dictionary. "We didn't quite know what was wearing us down the most," Ernaux recalls of that period: "the media and their opinion polls, who do you trust, their condescending comments, the politicians with their promises to reduce unemployment and plug the hole in the social security budget, or the escalator at the RER station that was always out of order."

A decade of populist turmoil later, Ernaux's testimony appears both familiar and unfamiliar. The rapid individualization and decline of collective institutions she observed has not been halted. Barring a few exceptions, political parties have not regained their members. Associations have not seen attendance rise. Churches have not filled their pews, and unions have not resurrected themselves. Around the world, civil society is still mired in a deep and protracted crisis, with what passes for political action monopolized by flash mobs, NGOs, and philanthropists with weak democratic mandates and nonexistent membership bases. The American political sociologist Theda Skocpol rightly describes a combination of "heads without bodies" and "bodies without heads."

On the other hand, the mixture of diffidence and apathy so characteristic of Ernaux's 1990s hardly applies today. The Brexit referendum was the largest democratic vote in Britain's history; President Joe Biden was elected by a record turnout. The Black Lives Matter protests were mass events, and many of the world's largest corporations took up the mantra of racial justice, adapting their brands to support the cause. Platforms like TikTok, YouTube, and Twitter are bursting with political content, from vloggers declaiming socialist pamphlets to right-wing influencers snarling about refugees. A new form of "politics" is visible on NBA courts and NFL fields, in the most popular Netflix shows, and in the labels with which people describe themselves on their social media pages.

To many on the right, society now feels overwhelmed by a permanent Dreyfus Affair—spilling over into family dinners, friends' drinks, and workplace lunches. To people who consider themselves centrists, it has created a longing for an era before the new hyper-politics, a nostalgia for post-history in the 1990s and 2000s, when markets and technocrats were exclusively in charge of policy. That era of "post-politics" has clearly ended. Yet instead of a rekindling of the politics of the twentieth century—complete with a revival of mass parties, unions, and workplace militancy—it is almost as if a step has been skipped.

Those who were politicized by the era surrounding the financial crash will remember a time when nothing, not even the austerity policies imposed in its wake, could be described as political. Today, everything is political, and fervently so. And yet, despite these wild passions overtaking and remaking some of the West's most powerful institutions—particularly in the United States—very few people are involved in the kind of organized conflict between interests that we might once have described as politics in its classical, twentieth-century sense, and antipolitical sentiment has not declined. The resulting hybrid may feel both inspiring and exasperating, but it has not produced the renaissance of class politics which the populist left originally wanted to kick-start.

To understand the shift from post-politics to hyper-politics, it is worth recalling the shape of the interregnum we're leaving. In the years after 2008, the political ice age that had followed the collapse of the Berlin Wall began steadily to thaw. Across the West—from Occupy Wall Street in the United States to 15-M in Spain and antiausterity fervor in Britain—movements began to emerge that once more raised the specter of competing interests. They did not happen within the formal realms of politics, however, and their "neither right nor left" rhetoric was sometimes seen as antipolitical. Yet they nonetheless marked the end of an era of consensus.

Across this populist explosion, organizational alternatives to the old mass party model proliferated. Movements, NGOs, corporations, and polling companies, with names like Extinction Rebellion or the Brexit Party, today offer more flexible models than the working-class parties of yore, which are now perceived as too sluggish for politicians and citizens alike. The people who would have once been party members can now opt out of enlisting in long-term, involuntary associations, while politicians are supposedly met with less resistance at their party congresses.

Strange new political forms have since taken the mass party's place. So-called digital parties—from La France insoumise and Podemos on the left to Macron's La République en marche! in the center and Italy's Five Star Movement somewhere in between—promised less bureaucracy, increased participation, and new modes of horizontal politics. In reality, they mostly delivered concentrated power for the personalities around which their projects had been built. French far-right candidate Éric Zemmour goes on millennial talk shows, while Dutch politicians hold Twitch streaming sessions. As vehicles, parties are slowly dying out or being replaced by cadre organizations. The rest of the party is then retrained as tribunes.

Electoral opportunism is certainly part of the driving force behind this new "movementism." For most European parties, the recent conversion to the movement model takes place against the backdrop of a double shift—a long-term decline in the number of party members and a continuous shrinkage in their electorate. Belgium offers a poignant example of this trend. The Flemish Christian Democrats still had an impressive 130,000 members in 1990; they now count a meager 43,000. In the same period, the Flemish Socialists plummeted from 90,000 to 10,000.[2] Almost everywhere, a similar story plays out: the former mass party lives on as a supplier of policy (what political scientists call democracy's "output factor"), but internally, it is eaten up by PR specialists and functionaries. Ernaux's memoir recounts how the very headquarters of the Socialist Party, which she voted for in 1981, were put up for sale in 2017, after the socialists were left stranded in fifth place in the country's presidential elections. Taking stock of defeat, the populist left repoliticized and even British Conservatives have now been coaxed into using developmental rhetoric, with Boris Johnson explicitly calling for a return to "one-nation conservatism," the Tory tradition of free-market skepticism. COVID-19 has also dynamited parts of the neoliberal consensus. Governments across the Western world are approaching

World War II levels of deficit spending, while the fiscal dam has been broken from Singapore to Budapest. Apart from in China, however, the Western states have taken on a curiously double role in the new statist moment. Welfarism in the twentieth century constituted an experimental program in a mixed economy alongside national development. Spurred on by a fractious but organized coalition between labor and small business, states invested in long-term public services, the electrification of rural areas, and the building of dams, roads, bridges, and other infrastructure. In that era's most ambitious moments, public money was spent on building public goods, with little private-sector involvement.

This type of remaking of the economy for the public good has been, so far, completely absent from COVID crisis fighting. Instead, policymakers have opted to replace the invisible hand of the market with the invisible hand of the state—a referee who will occasionally assist the players but rarely, if ever, participate in the game itself. In the meantime, the types of popular mobilization that originally fomented the creation of these welfare states has been inconstant or stymied by reigning party cadres. Unsurprisingly, the Starmerite counterrevolution within the UK Labour Party has focused on targeting members and their powers: if the party is to be made into another vehicle for professional politics, members must be disempowered, incentivized to leave, or outright expelled. With more than 150,000 having already departed, that process is well underway.

The lessons for left populists were bitter enough. While most of the left breakthroughs of recent years (from Syriza to Podemos and La France insoumise) have sought to express themselves in the form of new organizations, Corbynism was probably the last effort to reinvigorate the stodgy working-class parties of the past. The Flemish socialist leader, Conner Rousseau, recently celebrated the party's new look by welcoming a fresh "start-up atmosphere" within it and showing off his follower count on Instagram. Indeed, parties now regularly put out calls for "social media managers" and spread their messages through influencers; Macron recently hosted two YouTube vloggers at the presidential palace. In the final analysis, these new digital parties and the movements that spawned them were less negations of the post-industrial economy than expressions of it—highly informal and impermanent, avoiding long contracts, arranged around fleeting start-ups and ventures.

Of course, the low exit costs of these projects are eminently compatible with the mobile lifestyles of networked middle classes. Citizens who roam from temporary employment to temporary employment find it harder to build lasting relationships in their workplaces. Instead, a smaller circle of family, friends, and online connections now offers a more reliable social environment. Two poles respectively promote the most concrete and the most abstract types of solidarity—families as private insurance funds, and the internet as an entirely voluntary social arena.

This voluntarism finds clear resonances in the persistent mood of protest so endemic to contemporary politics. On the surface, there would seem to be little that unites the Black Lives Matter protests with QAnon or the January 6 riots in Washington, DC. Certainly, in moral terms, they are worlds apart—one protesting police brutality and racism, the other obsessed with fictitious electoral fraud and conspiracy theories. Organizationally, however, such movements are similar: they do not have membership lists; they have difficulty imposing discipline on their followers; and they do not formalize themselves into organizations.

Political theorist Paolo Gerbaudo has described the new protest movements with reference to Deleuze and Guattari's "bodies without organs"—clenched and muscular, but with no real internal metabolism, subject to constant constipation and impotence. It is no wonder that such a fluid form of authoritarianism, calling on presidents to cancel elections and sidestep parliaments, should chime harmoniously with today's stagnant service economies. An age of changing employment contracts and growing self-employment does not stimulate solid, lasting bonds within organizations. In the mass party's place has come a curious combination of the horizontal and the hierarchical, with leaders who manage a loose group of loyalists without ever imposing a clear party line or discipline.

Works such as the Austrian writer Elias Canetti's *Crowds and Power*, originally conceived in interwar Vienna, already recognized this type of leaderism. Canetti's classic text was composed in reaction to the great worker uprisings of the 1930s. The interwar workers' movement provoked an aggressive right-wing riposte in the form of fascism, and the period ultimately came down to two organized mass movements—fascism and communism—facing off against each other. Rather than a mobile "mass," today's QAnon troops and antilockdown protests look more like the infamous swarms: a group responding to short and powerful stimuli, driven by charismatic influencers and digital demagogues—the power to irritate, maybe a few stings here and there, but little more. Anyone can join a Facebook group with QAnon sympathies; as with all online media, the price of membership is very low, the cost of exit even lower. Leaders can, of course, try to choreograph these swarms—with tweets, television appearances, or supposed Russian bots. But that choreography still does not summon up a durable organization. This remains a decisive, yet also unstable, shift from mass-based party democracy. Whereas post-war parties had a tight team of midfielders and defenders, the new populist parties are mainly built around their star players. Its setup laid bare how social democracy's original dilemma—the trade-off between working and middle classes, which Kautsky, Gramsci, and Gorz had all sought to solve—had undergone an even more confusing mutation in the twenty-first century, enhanced by new dilemmas of demobilization first diagnosed in the 1990s. Left populists bravely reopened these questions but were unable to answer them.

It is not clear how this populist impulse will be channeled into our new era of public-private protectionism. The more the business of "government" gets left to the central banks, and the more economic policy relies on cash transfers, the less socialists have to offer as a philosophical counter-vision ("vote with your dollars or euros" seems to be the mantra of the future). If central banks can maintain certain consumption levels, the enormous gaps in inequality, the cannibalization of public services, and the decay of our social infrastructure can continue. Instead of reinvigorating the post-war welfare state, the COVID-19 pandemic opened the gateway to a "disinhibited

public-private project," as Adam Tooze recently put it.[3] The
vaccine race was itself a monument to this enterprise: the state
channels the cash, while companies plan and produce.

Yet the real lesson that has been learned from the "post-
political" era is that a modicum of deliberation over collective
ends cannot be kept out of the public sphere forever. Without
the re-emergence of mass organization, this can only occur at
a discursive level, arbitrated by media: every major event is
scrutinized for its ideological character, producing controver-
sies that play out among ever more clearly delineated camps
on social media platforms and are then rebounded through
each side's preferred media outlets. One with its age, populism
thereby revealed itself as a tragically transitory form of politics,
tied to a specific electoral cycle and subject to the passing hype
of a market society. In the twentieth century, it was hard to
speak of a Christian-Democratic or communist "moment" as
parties tied members to them for life and ministers bided their
time across decades. In contrast, the left's populist episode took
place in a political sphere increasingly oriented on short-term
gains and awash with exit options. The year 2008 did dynamite
the post-political consensus of the 1990s—an operation which
proved partly of left populism's valiant own doing. "The rumor
that politics was dead," as reported by Ernaux, now appears
muted. Hyper-politics offer us a fragile, petulant alternative
to the mass politics we knew in the twentieth century. Left
populism at least tried to resuscitate the latter. The first psycho-
analyst recognized this reflex all too well. The remarkable thing
about melancholy, according to Freud, was its tendency to
"turn into mania"—a "circular insanity" in which the patient

is afflicted by "constant fluctuations between melancholic and manic phases," both "struggling with the same complex": the "loss of the libidinous object." Ernaux, too, recognized that something was in danger of being lost. At the end of her book, she called on her readers to "save something from the time that will never be again"—but which apparently is not completely lost, either.

NOTES

1 Adam Przeworski, *Capitalism and Social Democracy*, Cambridge: Cambridge University Press, 1985.

2 Slavoj Žižek, "Against the Populist Temptation," *Critical Inquiry* 32 (Spring 2006).

3 Cited in Eric Hamburger, *John Reed*, London: Manchester University Press, 1990, p. 108.

4 Karl Kautsky, "Bauernagitation in Amerika," *Die Neue Zeit* 20/2 (1902): p. 463.

5 Dylan Riley's foreword in Nicos Poulantzas, *Fascism and Dictatorship: The Third International and the Problem of Fascism*, London: Verso Books, 2019, p. xli.

6 Peter Mair, *Ruling the Void: The Hollowing of Western Democracy*, London: Verso Books, 2011.

7 Matthew Karp, "Party and Class in American Politics: Reply to Riley and Brenner's 'Seven Theses,'" *New Left Review* II/139 (2023).

8 Ernesto Laclau, *On Populist Reason*, London: Verso Books, 2005; Chantal Mouffe and Ernesto Laclau, *Hegemony and Socialist Strategy*, London: Verso Books, 1985.

9 Ekaitz Cancela and Pedro M. Rey-Araújo, "Lessons of the Podemos Experiment," *New Left Review* II/138 (2022): p. 129.

10 Paolo Gerbaudo, "The Age of the Hyperleader: When Political Leadership Meets Social Media Celebrity," *New Statesman*, March 8, 2019.

11 Adam Tooze, *Shutdown: How Covid Shook the World's Economy*, New York: Penguin Press, 2021, p. 32.

12   René Rojas, "The Latin American Left's Shifting Tides," *Catalyst* 2/2 (2018).

13   Dylan Riley, "Bernstein's Heirs," *New Left Review* II/76 (2012): p. 150.

1. What Is Populism?

1   "Tectonique des politiques," Interview with Marcel Gauchet, *France Culture*, October 4, 2021.

2   Jan-Werner Müller, *What Is Populism?*, Philadelphia: University of Pennsylvania Press, 2016.

3   Federico Tarragoni, *L'esprit démocratique du populisme*, Paris: La Découverte, 2019.

4   Cas Mudde, "The Populist Zeitgeist," *Government and Opposition* 39/4 (2004).

5   Yascha Mounk, *The People vs. Democracy: Why Our Freedom Is in Danger and How to Save It*, Cambridge, MA, and London: Harvard University Press, 2018.

6   "Stephen Bannon, l'étoile noire de Donald Trump," *Le Monde*, December 18, 2016.

7   Marco D'Eramo, "Populism and the New Oligarchy," *New Left Review* 82 (2013).

8   Ignatius Donnelly, "The Omaha Platform [of the National People's Party]," in George Brown Tindall (ed.), *A Populist Reader: Selections from the Works of American Populist Leaders*, New York: Harper and Row, 1966, p. 91.

9   Cited in Gary Marotta, "Richard Hofstadter's Populist Problem and His Identity as a Jewish Intellectual," in John Abromeit et al. (eds.), *Transformations of Populism in Europe and the Americas*, London: Bloomsbury, 2016, p. 119.

10   Saul Bellow, *It All Adds Up: From the Dim Past to the Uncertain Future*, New York: Penguin Press, 1994, p. 102.

11   George B. Tindall, "Populism: A Semantic Identity Crisis," *Virginia Quarterly Review* 48 (1972): p. 501.

12   Pierre-André Taguieff, "La rhétorique du national-populisme (II)," *Mots* 9 (1984).

13   Stuart Hall, "Popular Democratic vs. Authoritarian Populism: Two Ways of Taking Democracy Seriously," in Alan Hunt (ed.), *Marxism and Democracy*, London: Lawrence and Wishart, 1980, pp. 160–1.

14   G. M. Tamás, "The Mystery of 'Populism' Finally Unveiled," *openDemocracy*, February 24, 2017.

15   Oliver Eagleton, "What Chantal Mouffe Gets Wrong," *New Statesman*, November 29, 2022. See also Perry Anderson, *The H-Word: The Peripeteia of Hegemony*, London: Verso Books, 2017.

16   Charles Postel, *The Populist Vision*, New York: Oxford University Press, 2007.

2. Why Populism?

1   Paolo Gerbaudo, *The Mask and the Flag: Populism, Citizenism and Global Protest*, London: Hurst and Company, 2017, pp. 56–9.

2   David Broder, *First They Took Rome: How the Populist Right Conquered Italy*, London and New York: Verso, 2020, p. 91.

3   Colin Crouch, *The Strange Non-Death of Neoliberalism*, Malden, MA: Polity, 2011.

4   This is what Colin Crouch referred to as "privatized Keynesianism": a system in which the internal demand was artificially sustained through credit rather than wage increase. Colin Crouch, "Privatised Keynesianism: An Unacknowledged Policy Regime," *British Journal of Politics and International Relations* 11/3 (2009).

5   Wolfgang Streeck, *Buying Time: The Delayed Crisis of Democratic Capitalism*, London and New York: Verso, 2014.

6   Girolamo Santocono, *La rue des Italiens*, Mons: Editions du Cerisier, 1986, p. 13.

7   Raúl Guillén, "À Madrid, des vies 'sous hypothèque'," *Manière de voir* 119 (2011): 56.

8   José Luis Zapatero, "Entrevista al presidente del Gobierno en el programa 'Herrera en la onda,' de Onda Cero," Madrid, January 4, 2011.

9   Lucia Quaglia and Sebastián Rojo, "Banks and the political economy of the sovereign debt crisis in Italy and Spain," *Review of International Political Economy* 22, 3 (2015): p. 500.

10   Mark Blyth, *Austerity: The History of a Dangerous Idea*, New York: Oxford University Press, 2013.

11   Mario Monti, "Transcript of PM Monti's intervention at the 2nd Tommaso Padoa-Schioppa Lecture, Brussels Economic Forum," Brussels, May 31, 2012.

12 Mariano Rajoy, "Conferencia de prensa del presidente del Gobierno," Madrid, August 3, 2012.

13 Broder, *First They Took Rome*, p. 83.

14 Richard Heuzé, "Interview with Mario Monti: 'Italie, souffrir pour guérir'," *Politique international* 137 (2012).

15 Cited in Broder, *First They Took Rome*, p. 106.

16 Armin Schäfer and Wolfgang Streeck (eds.), *Politics in the Age of Austerity*, Cambridge: Polity Press, 2013, p. 1.

17 Yanis Varoufakis, *Adults in the Room: My Battle with Europe's Deep Establishment*, New York: Vintage Books, 2018.

18 Marie Jahoda, Paul Lazarsfeld, and Hans Zeisel, *Marienthal: The Sociography of an Unemployed Community*, New York: Aldine, 1971, p. 16.

19 Cited in Renato Cristi, *Carl Schmitt and Authoritarian Liberalism: Strong State, Free Economy*, Cardiff: University of Wales Press, 1998, p. 196.

20 G. M. Tamás, "Telling the Truth about Class," *Socialist Register* (2006): p. 9.

21 "And what does one call a country that has as its president a military man with plenipotentiary powers, a secret police, a single television channel and whose entire information system is controlled by the state? I call it France, and not just any France, the France of General de Gaulle." Cited in ouest-france.fr/citation-film-oss-117-rio-ne-repond-plus.

22 Martin Conway, *Western Europe's Democratic Age: 1945–1968*, New York: Princeton University Press, 2022.

23 Matt Karp, "The Politics of a Second Gilded Age," *Jacobin*, February 17, 2021.

24 Theda Skocpol, "Advocates without Members: The Recent Transformation of American Civic Life," in in Theda Skocpol and Morris P. Fiorina (eds.), *Civic Engagement in American Democracy*, Washington, DC: Brookings Institution Press, 1999. See also Benjamin Fong and Melissa Naschek, "NGOism: The Politics of the Third Sector," *Catalyst* 5:1 (Spring 2021).

25 Christopher J. Bickerton and Carlo Invernizzi Accetti, *Technopopulism: The New Logic of Democratic Politics*, London: Oxford University Press, 2021; Vivien A. Schmidt, *Democracy in Europe: The EU and National Polities*, New York: Oxford University Press, 2006.

26 Christopher Hitchens, *For the Sake of Argument: Essays and Minority Reports*, London: Verso Books, 1992, p. 161.

27 Michel Crozier, Samuel Huntington et al., *The Crisis of Democracy:*

Report on the Governability of Democracies to the Trilateral Commission, New York: New York University Press, 1975, p. 9.

28 Streeck, *Buying Time*.

29 Mancur Olson, *The Logic of Collective Action*, New York: Harvard University Press, 1972, p. 166.

30 James Heartfield, "The Failure of the Capitalist Class and the Retreat from Production," *Platypus Review* 70 (October 2014).

31 Jean-Claude Michéa, "À voix nue: La chance d'avoir des parents communistes," *France Culture*, January 7, 2019.

32 Yohann Koshy, "Cappuccino-gate, or The Crisis of Authentocracy," *Le monde diplomatique* (2018); Joe Kennedy, *Authentocrats: Culture, Politics and the New Seriousness*, London: Repeater Books, 2018.

33 Stephanie Mudge, *Leftism Reinvented: Western Parties from Socialism to Neoliberalism*, New York: Harvard University Press, 2018; Mark Bovens and Anchrit Wille, *Diploma Democracy: The Rise of Political Meritocracy*, London: Oxford University Press, 2017.

3. Ebb and Flow

1 "Union Populaire" was the name of the organization Mélenchon built around his own presidential campaign; the NUPES label was coined only after the presidential election to name the electoral coalition between *les insoumis*, socialists, greens, and communists in the parliamentary election.

2 Adam Tooze, *Crashed: How a Decade of Financial Crises Changed the World*, New York: Viking, 2018, pp. 330–1.

3 Enrico Padoan, *Anti-Neoliberal Populisms in Comparative Perspective: A Latinamericanisation of Southern Europe?* New York and London: Routledge, 2021, pp. 240–1.

4 Giorgios Katsambekis, "The Populist Radical Left in Greece: Syriza," in Giorgios Katsambekis and Alexandros Kioupkiolis, *The Populist Radical Left in Europe*, London and New York: Routledge, 2019, p. 26.

5 Adapted from an interview with Djordje Kuzmanovic, ex-member and international secretary of LFI, conducted on December 11, 2020.

6 "Grèce: un revolver sur la tempe," Jean-Luc Mélenchon's blog, July 13, 2015, melenchon.fr.

7   Yanis Varoufakis, "Leur seul objectif était de nous humilier," *Le Monde diplomatique*, August 2015.

8   Gérard Mauger, "Un pistolet sur la tempe," *Savoir/Agir* 34:4 (2015).

9   Katsambekis, "The Populist Radical Left in Greece," p. 36; Grigoris Markou, "Populism in Government: The Case of SYRIZA (2015–2019)," in Pierre Ostiguy et al. (eds.), *Populism in Global Perspective: A Performative and Discursive Approach*, London and New York: Routledge, 2021, p. 182.

10   Stathis Kouvelakis, "Syriza's Failure Has Hurt Us All," *Jacobin*, June 11, 2019.

11   Yanis Varoufakis, "Syriza Was a Bigger Blow to the Left Than Thatcher," *Jacobin*, March 9, 2020.

12   Giorgos Venizelos and Yannis Stavrakakis, "Left-Populism Is Down but Not Out," *Jacobin*, March 22, 2020.

13   "El Partido Popular insta al 15-M a conseguir sus objetivos 'con votos, no sólo con pancartas'," *Público*, May 14, 2013.

14   Heriberto Rodríguez Hernández, "Política, Manual de Instrucciones," 2016, vimeo.com.

15   Paula Biglieri and Luciana Cadahia, *Seven Essays on Populism*, Cambridge: Polity Press, 2021.

16   Pablo Iglesias, *Politics in a Time of Crisis: Podemos and the Future of European Democracy*, London and New York: Verso, 2015, pp. 11–8.

17   Interview with Pierre K., Zoom, December 4, 2020.

18   Manuel Cervera-Marzal, *Le populisme de gauche. Sociologie de la France insoumise*, Paris: La Découverte, 2021.

19   Ibid.

4. Populist Postgame

1   Eric Hobsbawm, "The Forward March of Labour Halted?," *Marxism Today* (1978).

2   Stuart Hall, *The Hard Road to Renewal: Thatcherism and the Crisis of the Left*, London: Verso Books, 2021, p. 205. See also Ellen Meiksins Wood, *The Retreat from Class*, London: Verso Books, 1986.

3   Paolo Gerbaudo, *The Digital Party: Political Organisation and Online Democracy*, London, Pluto Press, 2019, p. 151.

4   Ibid., pp. 150–60.

5   Matt Bolton, "The Terrifying Hubris of Corbynism," *Medium*, July 14, 2016.

6   "Research Briefing: Membership of political parties in Great Britain," House of Commons Library, August 30, 2022, researchbriefings.files.parliament.uk/.

7   This hostility towards political mediation, although widely shared by the new political challengers that thrive in the post-mass parties era, stems from various sources, ranging from the most personal to the most ideologically driven aversion. Whereas Mélenchon's rejection of the classic party form is related to his past experience as a member of the French socialists, the Five Star Movement borrows its antiparty sentiments from a long-standing tradition of liberal hostility toward factionalism and, more specifically, to authors such as Simone Weil and Adriano Olivetti.

8   "Huge legal bills leave Labour feeling the pinch," *The Times*, July 24, 2021.

9   Cervera-Marzal, *Le populisme de gauche*, p. 188.

10 "Podemos estrena su nuevo censo de militantes con 19,000 personas inscritas," *Europapress*, October 16, 2020.

11 See Rick Falkvinge, *Swarmwise: The Tactical Manual to Changing the World*, N. Charleston, SC: CreateSpace Publishing Platform, 2016, and Gerbaudo, *The Digital Party*.

12 Gerbaudo, *The Digital Party*, p. 171.

13 Cecilia Biancalana and Davide Vittori, "Cyber-Parties' Membership Between Empowerment and Pseudo-Participation: The Cases of Podemos and the Five Star Movement," in O. Barberà et al. (eds.), *Digital Parties: Studies in Digital Politics and Governance*, New York: Springer, 2021.

14 Gerbaudo, *The Digital Party*, p. 128.

5. Five Scenarios

1   Oliver Eagleton, *The Starmer Project*, London: Verso Books, 2022.

2   Bhaskar Sunkara, *The Socialist Manifesto: The Case for Radical Politics in an Era of Extreme Inequality*, London: Verso Books, 2019.

Conclusion

1   Annie Ernaux, *The Years*, London: Seven Stories Press, 2017, p. 191.

2   "Jan-Frederik Abbeloos, "Meer centen dan leden: waarom politieke parti-jen ondanks miljoenenuitgaven op Facebook met een groot probleem zitten," *De Standaard*, January 21, 2022.

3   John Terese, "Is This the Green New Deal?," *Damage Magazine*, September 14, 2021.